little book of big bible promises
for men

With God everything is possible.

Matthew 19:26

Contents

Introduction

In the middle of a problem have you ever thought you needed a "help finder" just for men to help locate encouragement for a particular situation or set of circumstances?

Here it is! A book for men who understand that the Bible offers advice and comfort for many of the problems encountered in today's world but don't know where in the Bible to find it. We yearn for some relief from worry, some comfort, some bit of assurance in the middle of a muddle. But so often we locate just the right Scripture "after the fact" and then wish we could have found it yesterday. This book will help with that.

We cannot expect to have the wind at our backs all the way to heaven. Every man needs answers to questions such as "Why me?" or "Will God take me back when I've strayed?" At one time or another, each of us needs help in decision making. We need extra strength to keep on keeping on under stress or when burn-out takes over. Is there a man anywhere who honestly believes he has enough of God's wisdom to handle his corner of this unstable and ever changing world? God did not place us here on Planet Earth without direction and instruction. And it is in easy-to-understand written form! God has been faithful throughout history to make and keep his promises, to guide and to comfort, even in this sophisticated age. Today his promises give us insight to work through decisions and problems with calm and wisdom. God wants us to seek out these comforting promises and to pursue them persistently, but most of all to claim them as our own. But, how can we claim these encouraging helps if we are unaware of them?

That is what this book is for—to lead men to specific extraordinary parts of the Bible where there is help for a particular problem when the storms of life blow.

When a man's heart and mind are focused on God and his Word, he develops hope and calm trust that things are under control. Inspiring Bible words can bring that elusive and consistent peace that so many today are seeking but so few seem to have found.

You can let God's promises shine on your problems. Using this book, you can run to his comforting words to help you swim through your barrage of troubles and temptations, however large or small they may be.

God makes promises and keeps them.

when a man has a hard
decision to make

Mind-Renewal Thought

I Can Go to the Lord for Help

The Lord says, "I will guide you along the best pathway for your life. I will advise you and watch over you."

PSALM 32:8

Thinking It Over

God loves to be consulted.

—Charles Bridges

TAKEAWAY

All the way my Savior leads me;
What have I to ask beside?
Can I doubt His tender mercy,
Who through life has been my guide?
Heav'nly peace, divinest comfort,
Here by faith in Him to dwell!
For I know whate'er befall me,
Jesus doeth all things well.

—Fanny Jane Crosby (1820–1915)

Mind-Renewal Thought

I Can Ask Godly Friends for Advice

The heartfelt counsel of a friend is as sweet as perfume and incense. . . . As iron sharpens iron, a friend sharpens a friend.

PROVERBS 27:9, 17

Thinking It Over

When we have blind spots, God often raises up people to come alongside us as counselors. Being open to ideas from outside, especially when making a difficult decision, is a trait of an intelligent person. To confirm this truth, read Psalm 37:30.

Do you have a trusted godly friend to whom you can go for advice? The advice of the wise can be a life-giving fountain.

TAKEAWAY

George Washington hated conflicts and quarrels and wanted a united Cabinet. Yet he made quite sure of the necessary differences of opinion on important matters by asking both Hamilton and Jefferson for their opinions.

—Peter Drucker

Mind-Renewal Thought

I Can Search the Scriptures for Wisdom

Your word stands firm in heaven. . . .
Your laws remain true today. . . . Your commands are my constant guide. . . . Your word is a lamp for my feet and a light for my path.

PSALM 119:89, 91, 98, 105

Thinking It Over

It's Not So Hard to Make Decisions
If Our Values Are Clear

God is not silent when life seems confusing and we don't know which road to take. He has spoken through his Word, through that very Bible on your coffee table or stashed in the closet. Knowing the Scriptures helps keep our spiritual bearings in the midst of chaos.

Gleaning their wisdom gives more options in our decision making and provides us with the discernment we need to make healthy choices. Let's not forget the basics: A right decision is one that is consistent with the principles of truth found in God's Word.

TAKEAWAY 

The wise man is also the just, the pious, the upright, the man who walks in the way of truth. The fear of the Lord, which is the beginning of wisdom, consists in a complete devotion to God.

—Otto Zockler (1775)

Mind-Renewal Thought

Which Option Honors God's Name Best?

Whatever [I] do, [I] must do all for the glory of God.

1 CORINTHIANS 10:31

Thinking It Over

The Christian's aim in life is to live for God's glory. If his goods be spoiled, he says, "If it glorifies God for me to lose my property, I am no loser. I gave my goods to God years ago." If he is put in prison, he says, "I have lost my liberty, but I am no loser. I gave up my liberty to God long ago." If they tell him that he will die, he says, "I am no loser for I gave him my life long ago. I am altogether Christ's." As the Prophet says: "Our heart's desire is to glorify your name" (Isaiah 26:8).

—Charles H. Spurgeon (1834–1892)

TAKEAWAY

Direct, control, suggest, this day
All I design or do or say,
That all my powers with all their might
In Thy sole glory may unite.

—Bishop Thomas Ken (1637–1711)

Day five

Mind-Renewal Thought

Making Decisions with Confidence

The Spirit of God . . . lives in you. . . . All who are led by the Spirit of God are children of God. So you should not be like cowering, fearful slaves. You should behave instead like God's very own children, adopted into his family—calling him "Father, dear Father."

ROMANS 8:11, 14-15

Thinking It Over

How-To

Once you have made up your mind, a lot of the stress will cease. Instead of worrying about what to do, set aside a time to be quiet, to become acutely aware of the Holy Spirit in you. Meditate on Jesus until you feel his presence in your innermost soul. Determine that you, as a man of God, actually are a child of God and that with the help of Scripture and wise and godly friends, you do have everything you need to make the best decision. Be sure you really expect the Holy Spirit to guide you, because a doubting mind is as unsettled as a wave of the sea.

Now, use your mind to contemplate choices, consider, plan, compare, and prepare as God leads. Write down the pros and cons of each choice so they are in front of you. Remind yourself who you are (God's child), and praise your Father aloud for the closeness of his help. Then, go forward with your decision in confidence knowing you have done the best you can. Leave the outcome to God and know that whatever happens, he can make good of it.

TAKEAWAY

In forty hours I shall be in battle, with little information, and on the spur of the moment will have to make the most momentous decisions. But I believe that one's spirit enlarges with responsibility and that, with God's help, I shall make them, and make them right.

—General George S. Patton (1885–1945)

Day. SIX

Mind-Renewal Thought

For Faint-Hearted Decision Makers

If you wait for perfect conditions, you will never get anything done.

ECCLESIASTES 11:4

Thinking It Over

Neil Simon once said, "If no one ever took risks, Michelangelo would have painted the Sistine floor." Fear of failure leads many to delay decisions endlessly and to sometimes do nothing at all when, in fact, something needs to be done. Inaction can create a problem for you and God. Wouldn't he rather see you go forward in confidence, trusting him? Scripture says, "Be strong and of good courage, and do it: fear not, nor be dismayed: for the Lord God, even my God, will be with thee; he will not fail thee, nor forsake thee" (1 Chronicles 28:20, KJV). The final word: Peter couldn't walk on the water until he got out of the boat. Neither can you.

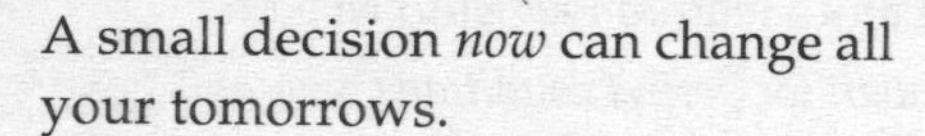

TAKEAWAY

A small decision *now* can change all your tomorrows.

—Robert Schuller (1926–)

When you have a serious decision to make, tell yourself firmly you are going to make it. Do not expect it will be the perfect one. Some of those "againsts" may never be canceled out. You must simply try to make the best decision you can, having taken all the "pros" and "cons" you can discover into account. Whether we like it or not, making a choice is a part of being human, and we do not think too highly of those who throw away this right—always needing someone else to make up their minds for them.

—*Woman's Weekly*

Day
seven

Mind-Renewal Thought

Transferring My Dependency to God

We can gather our thoughts, but the Lord gives the right answer. . . . Commit your work to the Lord, and then your plans will succeed.

PROVERBS 16:1, 3

Thinking It Over

I thought about divorce. My problem was what to do about a wonderful but stubborn wife who was difficult to deal with nearly every time a major family decision had to be made. There never seemed to be room for discussion. Whatever decision came to her mind and was uttered, good or bad, remained firmly entrenched in stone, even if it later became evident she might be wrong. For years she would never admit she was mistaken or change her mind. What to do? I tried for years to change this destructive stubbornness and to reason with her, particularly when family decisions needed to be made, but over and over her unthinking judgments dealt especially harsh emotional blows to our children. Should I divorce and deprive my kids of the closeness of a mother? Then, I told God aloud in prayer that I could not change the stubbornness and domineering spirit of this otherwise good woman, and I asked him to intervene and exclaimed aloud my dependence on my heavenly Father. I determined to stop trying to reason with my wife. I would wait out deciding about divorce and watch to see if God would work to change things. My decision was to pray daily, sometimes hourly, and to commit our marriage relationship to him. After several months I watched with unbelief as my wife became more of a helpmate, a bit more mellow. She seemed more aware of how her strong and stubborn will hurt those around her. I was amazed to sometimes see her back off from strong opinions and begin to listen better to those of others before coming to important conclusions. God works in mysterious ways *if we let him.*

—Georgia husband, father of four

TAKEAWAY

There is nothing so small that we may honour God by asking His guidance of it, or insult Him by taking it into our own hands.

—John Ruskin (1819–1900)

POWERTHOUGHT

My bark is wafted to the strand
By breath divine;
And on the helm there rests a hand
Other than mine.

—Dean Alford

why me, lord?

Mind-Renewal Thought

How frail is humanity! How short is life, and how full of trouble!

Job 14:1

Thinking It Over

Maybe you feel as if life is closing in on you. The truth is that bad things happen to good (and bad) people. While dealing with a wave of trouble, it is most likely impossible to know the "why" of it. Life can only be understood "backwards," in retrospect, and then not always. This one thing is true—that God is love and whatever he allows in the lives of his children will be turned into some good. A good parent always wants the best for his child. As a parent, our heavenly Father is the best of the best. Have you remembered to ask, "Why me?" when considering the *good* gifts he has given you: talents such as singing, writing, speaking, or excelling at sports or teaching, or tangible gifts such as money, a roof overhead, or good health?

TAKEAWAY

The great thing, if one can, is to stop regarding all the unpleasant things as interruptions of one's "own" or "real" life. The truth is of course that what one calls the interruptions are precisely one's real life—the life God is sending one day by day.

—C. S. Lewis (1898–1963)

Mind-Renewal Thought

Others Asked, Why Me?

The angel of the Lord appeared to [Gideon] and said, "Mighty hero, the Lord is with you!"
"Sir," Gideon replied, "if the Lord is with us, why has all this happened to us? And where are all the miracles our ancestors told us about? Didn't they say, 'The Lord brought us up out of Egypt'? But now the Lord has abandoned us and handed us over to the Midianites."
Then the Lord turned to him and said, "Go with the strength you have and rescue Israel from the Midianites. I am sending you!"

JUDGES 6:12-14

Thinking It Over

Perhaps today will be the day you can let go of the urgent need for explanations and the craving to incessantly ask why or who is to blame for circumstances. In Diane Cole's book *After Great Pain,* she writes about the futility of our need to place blame for what happens to us: "The world bears you no grudge; it is the nature of life to leave us vulnerable."

TAKEAWAY

Of our troubles we must seek some other cause than God.

—Plato (422–347 B.C.)

Mind-Renewal Thought

David's Explanation for Trouble

I used to wander off until you disciplined me; but now I closely follow your word. You are good and do only good; teach me your principles. . . . The suffering you sent was good for me, for it taught me to pay attention to your principles. . . . You made me; you created me. Now give me the sense to follow your commands. . . . You disciplined me because I needed it. Now let your unfailing love comfort me.

PSALM 119:67-68, 71, 73, 75-76

Thinking It Over

You can advance farther in grace in one hour during a time of affliction than in many days during a time of consolation.

—Jean Eudes

TAKEAWAY

He giveth more grace when the burden grows greater;
He sendeth more strength when the labors increase.
To added affliction He addeth His mercy;
To multiplied trials, His multiplied peace.

—Annie Johnson Flint (1862–1932)

Mind-Renewal Thought

We know that all that happens to us is working for our good if we love God.

ROMANS 8:28, TLB

Thinking It Over

The saint knows not why he suffers as he does, yet he comprehends with a knowledge that passes knowledge that all is well.

—Oswald Chambers (1874–1917)

TAKEAWAY

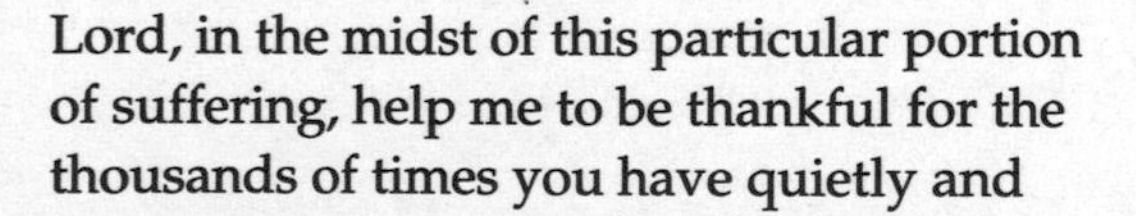

Lord, in the midst of this particular portion of suffering, help me to be thankful for the thousands of times you have quietly and secretly intervened and held back other afflictions or protected me from accidents in the past. And I never even knew! I take great comfort when I look back to see your faithfulness over and over in every crisis and chilling circumstance of my life. No wonder I love you so much. Thank you that only you know the beginning of things, the cause of things, and the end of things. When trouble breaks out, use it to mold and shape me into the image of your Son.

—A man suffering severe physical pain

Day five

Mind-Renewal Thought

Teaching My Children to Endure Difficulties with Dignity

All your sons will be taught by the Lord,
and great will be your children's peace.

Isaiah 54:13, NIV

Thinking It Over

My children are watching as I make choices about how I will respond to trials and difficulties. Like when that guy at work got the promotion that I thought I deserved, when I was stuck in traffic and late for work, or when there wasn't enough money at the end of the month to pay a bill or two after the washing machine quit running.

Lord, help me be to my children the kind of parent who models persistence and prayer in every trial and who trusts in you, no matter what happens. I want them to see you in me. In Jesus' name, amen.

TAKEAWAY

If you want your child to accept your values when he reaches his teen years, then you must be worthy of his respect during his younger days.

—Dr. James C. Dobson (1936–)

Day.
SIX

Mind-Renewal Thought

One Good Answer to "Why Me?"

He comforts us in all our troubles so that we can comfort others. When others are troubled, we will be able to give them the same comfort God has given us. . . . For when God comforts us, it is so that we, in turn, can be an encouragement.

2 CORINTHIANS 1:4, 6

Thinking It Over

Those who do not feel pain seldom think that it is felt.

—Samuel Johnson (1709–1784)

TAKEAWAY 

Blest be the tie that binds
Our hearts in Christian love:
The fellowship of kindred minds
Is like to that above.

We share each other's woes,
Our mutual burdens bear,
And often for each other flows
The sympathizing tear.

—John Fawcett (1740–1817)

Day
seven

Mind-Renewal Thought

Paul: A Reason for Adversity

I think you ought to know about the trouble we went through in the province of Asia. We were crushed and completely overwhelmed, and we thought we would never live through it. In fact, we expected to die. But as a result, we learned not to rely on ourselves, but on God.

2 CORINTHIANS 1:8-9

Thinking It Over

Life is full of people who "used to believe." But because things turned out darker and tougher than they supposed, they have decided that "there can't be a God to let things like that happen." But "things like that" have always happened, to all sorts of people; even to Christ. We simply do not know *why* life should, apparently, be so easy for one and so heartbreakingly difficult for another. Let's not pretend. No one *likes* pain or difficulty or this sense of darkness and being alone. But if we can accept it as a part of life and hold on to the God who, apparently, isn't there, we shall eventually emerge toughened and strengthened.

—J. B. Phillips (1906–1982)

TAKEAWAY

God, who foresaw your tribulation, has specially armed you to go through it, not without pain but without stain.

—C. S. Lewis (1898–1963)

POWERTHOUGHT

Christ's suffering at Calvary was always something I believed but never really felt . . . until I myself experienced terrible pain, unbearable suffering, in an awful car accident. Then, his pain became mine. Then the real meaning of 1 Peter 4:13 came clear: "Trials will make you partners with Christ in his suffering."

—A Florida man

when you are afraid of what lies ahead

Day one

Mind-Renewal Thought

The Lord is for me, so I will not be afraid.
What can mere mortals do to me? Yes, the Lord
is for me; he will help me. . . . It is better to trust the
Lord than to put confidence in people. It is better
to trust the Lord than to put confidence in princes.

PSALM 118:6-9

Thinking It Over

Let us be of good cheer, remembering that the misfortunes hardest to bear are those which never come.

—James Russell Lowell (1819–1891)

TAKEAWAY 

Antidote for Fear

Write the following Scripture verses on a note card for the next time you find yourself afraid of what is going to happen. Say the verses aloud with conviction five times whenever you need encouragement and courage. You may even want to raise your hands to the One who has your future in his hands!

> *I am trusting you, O Lord, saying, "You are my God!" My future is in your hands. . . . Let your favor shine on your servant. . . . My heart is confident in you, O God. . . . Your unfailing love is as high as the heavens. Your faithfulness reaches to the clouds.* (Psalm 31:14-16; 57:7,10)

Mind-Renewal Thought

Even God's Great Men Were Sometimes Afraid

Fear and trembling overwhelm me. I can't stop shaking. Oh, how I wish I had wings like a dove; then I would fly away and rest! I would fly away to the quiet of the wilderness. . . . But I will call on God. Morning, noon, and night I plead aloud in my distress. . . . God, who is king forever, will hear me.

PSALM 55:5-7, 16-19

Thinking It Over

Fear is the pain before the wound.

—Noah ben Shea

TAKEAWAY

To rest in the Lord means to trust in him, to be convinced that whatever he has in store for you absolutely and unquestionably is in your best interests. Resting in the Lord is a key element. . . . If he is omnipotent and omniscient, then there is no way to improve upon his ways and timing.

—Dr. Charles Stanley

Mind-Renewal Thought

Those who live in the shelter of the Most High
will find rest in the shadow of the Almighty.
This I declare of the Lord: He alone is my refuge,
my place of safety; he is my God, and I am trusting
him. . . . He will shield you with his wings.
He will shelter you with his feathers.

PSALM 91:1-2, 4

Thinking It Over

The man of faith is never blind to the desolation. He sees clearly all the terrible facts. But he sees more. He sees God.

—G. Campbell Morgan (1863–1945)

TAKEAWAY

Begone, unbelief;
My Savior is near,
And for my relief
Will surely appear;
By prayer let me wrestle,
And he will perform;
With Christ in the vessel,
I smile at the storm.

—John Newton (1725–1807)

Mind-Renewal Thought

God is our refuge and strength, always ready to help in times of trouble. So we will not fear, even if earthquakes come and the mountains crumble into the sea. Let the oceans roar and foam. Let the mountains tremble as the waters surge! . . . The nations are in an uproar, and kingdoms crumble! God thunders, and the earth melts! The Lord Almighty is here among us; the God of Israel is our fortress.

PSALM 46:1-3, 6-7

Thinking It Over

Happy the child who in thunder-claps detects the Father's voice. There is no fear in love, because perfect love casteth out the fear that hath torment.

—F. B. Meyer (1847–1929)

TAKEAWAY

Our faith does not lie in trusting God to stop the storm but in trusting him to enable us to walk through the storm.

—Jill Briscoe

Day five

Mind-Renewal Thought

God Sends Angels as Helpers

He orders his angels to protect you wherever you go. They will hold you with their hands to keep you from striking your foot on a stone.

PSALM 91:11-12

Thinking It Over

God gets great pleasure from sending his agents on secret reconnaissance missions with personal instructions no one else knows about.

Bill Hybels (1951–)

TAKEAWAY

Seeing we are so dear to God, these angels take this charge upon them with all their hearts, and omit nothing in their duty from our birth to the end of our life.

—Henry Lawrence

Day. SIX

Mind-Renewal Thought

I have chosen you. . . . Don't be afraid, for I am with you. Do not be dismayed, for I am your God. I will strengthen you. I will help you. I will uphold you with my victorious right hand.

ISAIAH 41:9-10

Thinking It Over

Troubles will come to you sooner or later. . . . At those times you must hold fast to the fact that God makes no mistakes; He has not forgotten you.

—Jerry Falwell (1933–)

TAKEAWAY

Picture in your mind your loving heavenly Father standing beside you right now, wherever you are. His gentle hand is on your shoulder as you fret over your difficulties. Keep that thought at least sixty seconds. Can you see the compassion in his eyes, the tender smile on his face? Ask yourself whether it might be an insult to this loving God, who created the heavens and the earth simply by uttering a word, if you allow circumstances to bring terrible and destructive fear into your heart when you know he is fully committed to your care. Now ask yourself, *Wouldn't a good earthly father feel insulted and hurt if his beloved child said, "Dad, I do not trust you"?* Here is what God wants of a man when turbulence hits: "Trust me in your times of trouble, and I will rescue you, and you will give me glory" (Psalm 50:15).

Day seven

Mind-Renewal Thought

He is like a father to us, tender and sympathetic to those who reverence him. For he knows we are but dust, and that our days are few and brief, like grass, like flowers, blown by the wind and gone forever.

PSALM 103:13-16, TLB

Thinking It Over

Today is all any man has—this hour, this minute, this second. Entertaining what-ifs will dull and paralyze my mind with anxiety and spoil my time. Fearful living and being afraid of the future is not the abundant life God planned for me. He promised never to leave me alone or abandon me, yet I sometimes act as if the outcome of things depends on me alone.

No longer forward nor behind
I look in hope or fear;
But, grateful, take the good I find,
The best of now and here.

—John Greenleaf Whittier (1807–1892)

TAKEAWAY 

For Worried Moments

1. Take comfort in God's past faithfulness

   Through many dangers, toils and snares
   I have already come;
   'Tis grace hath brought me safe thus far,
   And grace will lead me home.

   —John Newton (1725–1807)

2. Look back on your life and recall one fearful event that you now see clearly how God's hand was in it. Record it here, then praise him for his help. Say aloud, "He was there all the time!" Now, read Psalm 77 and David's account of being rescued from his enemies in Psalm 18.

3. Say aloud: "When I am afraid, I put my trust in you" (Psalm 56:3).

POWERTHOUGHT

For Worried Moments

Since fear is unreasonable, never try to reason with it. So-called "positive thinking" is no weapon against fear. Only positive faith can rout the black menace of fear and give life a radiance.

—Marion Hilliard, *Digest of World Reading*

men under stress

Day one

Mind-Renewal Thought

For Men Who Can't Relax

A relaxed attitude lengthens [a man's] life.

PROVERBS 14:30

Thinking It Over

The nervous system of the body has two modes of operation. One is the *sympathetic nervous system,* which gets us ready for action: the fight or flight mode where most of the blood is in the muscles. This is also the mode where stress tenses back and neck muscles, and triggers asthma and migraines or heart attacks and strokes.

The second mode is the *parasympathetic nervous system,* [which] helps us relax, digest, and heal. We need both the action and repair modes but are often imbalanced by unrelenting stress.

To even yourself out through the day, do some (not random, but) *deliberate* acts of kindness. They are doubly healing for the giver and the receiver.

—Sherry Rogers, M.D.

TAKEAWAY

One way for a man to get his mind off tension and relieve stress is to focus on another person who might be enduring similar circumstances or worries. Begin to pray fervently for that individual and continue over days, even weeks.
A certain luster returns to life when we learn to pray for others as it diverts our minds from ourselves.

Day
two

Mind-Renewal Thought

Remembering God's Blessings Brings Relaxation and Joy

O God, my God! . . . Your love and kindness are better to me than life itself. How I praise you! . . . I lie awake at night thinking of you—of how much you have helped me—and how I rejoice!

PSALM 63:1, 3, 6-7, TLB

Thinking It Over

I remember one who, worn with sickness and sleepless nights, answered to the question if the nights did not seem interminable: "Oh no, I lie still and count my blessings."

—H. L. Sidney Lear

TAKEAWAY

So, amid the conflict, whether great or small,
Do not be discouraged, God is over all;
Count your many blessings, angels will attend,
Help and comfort give you to your journey's end.

—Johnson Oatman (1856–1922)

Mind-Renewal Thought

Setting the Mind on Positives Relaxes

Fix your thoughts on what is true and honorable and right. Think about things that are pure and lovely and admirable. Think about things that are excellent and worthy of praise.

PHILIPPIANS 4:8

Thinking It Over

In the name of God, stop a moment, cease your work, look around you.

—Leo Tolstoy (1828–1910)

TAKEAWAY

Dear God, our entire lives have been journeys of mercies and blessings shown to those most undeserving of them. Year after year you have carried us on, removed dangers from our paths, refreshed us, directed us, sustained us. We know you will stay with us, that we can rest assured in you. We may rest upon your arm; we can sleep like babies in their mothers' arms.

—John Henry Newman (1801–1890)

Mind-Renewal Thought

For Men Who Can't Relax

"Comfort, comfort my people," says your God.

ISAIAH 40:1

Thinking It Over

What have I to dread, what have I to fear,
Leaning on the everlasting arms?
I have blessed peace with my Lord so near,
Leaning on the everlasting arms.

—Elisha A. Hoffman (1839–1929)

TAKEAWAY

Don't be ashamed to be as a child in your relationship to God. Let the everlasting arms rock you to sleep. In complete trust, relax on God's amazing kindliness. He will take care of you day and night, forever.

—Dr. Norman Vincent Peale (1898–1993)

Day five

Mind-Renewal Thought

For Men Who Can't Relax

Sing a new song to the Lord! Sing his praises from the ends of the earth! Sing, all you who sail the seas, all you who live in distant coastlands. Join in the chorus! . . . Sing for joy!

ISAIAH 42:10-11

Thinking It Over

I sing (or whistle) stress away! When relaxation will not come, when worry overwhelms, when tension mounts, I get out a hymnbook, go by myself to a quiet place, and sing or just repeat the comforting words aloud. If no one can hear, I raise my baritone voice with enthusiasm, *never mind how I feel.* If I am in my office, where others might hear, I silently or quietly read the uplifting words to myself. It is the form of rest that relaxes me best.

—A Georgia businessman

TAKEAWAY

To sing stress away, try this stanza of the hymn "Praise the Lord! Ye Heavens Adore Him." Find rest in the God whose promises never fail.

Praise the Lord! For He is glorious;
Never shall His promise fail;
God hath made His saints victorious;
Sin and death shall not prevail.
Praise the God of our salvation!
Hosts on high, His pow'r proclaim;
Heav'n and earth and all creation,
Laud and magnify His name.

—*Foundling Hospital Collection*, 1796

Day.
SIX

Mind-Renewal Thought

For Men Who Can't Relax

God has said, "I will never fail you.
I will never forsake you." That is why
we can say with confidence,
"The Lord is my helper."

HEBREWS 13:5-6

Thinking It Over

God incarnate is the end of fear; and the heart that realizes that he is in the midst . . . will be quiet in the midst of alarm.

—F. B. Meyer (1847–1929)

TAKEAWAY 

When the pressures of our world mount, we are tempted to think that we have to "work things out on our own." While God does want us actively involved in the problem-solving process, his greater desire is for us to call out to him and declare our dependency on him. The psalmist writes, "God is our refuge and strength, a very present help in trouble" (Psalm 46:1, KJV). How can we right our upside-down world? There is a way. Begin with God. Spend time with him in prayer. You may think you can't afford to lose another minute, but you can't afford to miss the opportunity of allowing God to comfort you and provide the help you need.

—*In Touch*

Mind-Renewal Thoughts

Suggestions for Relieving Stress

Trust in the Lord and do good; dwell in the land and enjoy safe pasture. Delight yourself in the Lord and he will give you the desires of your heart.

PSALM 37:3-4, NIV

Thinking It Over

Languor is underrated. Bone-lazy idleness, hours spent staring at the sky and remembering books and birthdays and great kisses: this is a pure pleasure that eludes the productive in all their confident superiority. Languor is sunny and hot. It is at home near the sea and is appreciated in environments of beauty and limited promise. Fishing, for instance. But if you're always reeling in and checking your bait, you'll only worsen your chances.

—Kevin Patterson, *The Water In Between*

TAKEAWAY

When you're under pressure, when God hasn't removed the situations that overwhelm you despite your repeated begging, do something frivolous and nonstressful. Just get away for a while without really going anywhere. Throw a Frisbee with your dog or play catch with a child, rearrange your bookshelf, enter a contest, take a walk, drink a cup of hot chocolate, read a favorite poem or a chapter from the Psalms, whack a few weeds, look at the stars, hug your wife.

—A busy New York writer and editor

POWERTHOUGHT

A person is healed of burnout when he receives a fresh revelation of who God is.

—Malcolm Smith

will god forgive *that* sin?

Day one

Mind-Renewal Thought

Let there be tears for the wrong things you have done. Let there be sorrow and deep grief. . . . Bow down before the Lord and admit your dependence on him.

JAMES 4:9-10

Thinking It Over

Recognition of our wrongs is at least 90 percent of the battle. We have to acknowledge to God what we have done and ask him to forgive. What do you need to bring before the Lord right now? Come before him with your heart open to his grace and forgiveness.

Here is a wonderful Bible prayer for these times:

Have mercy on me, O God, because of your unfailing love. Because of your great compassion, blot out the stain of my sins. Wash me clean from my guilt. Purify me from my sin. For I recognize my shameful deeds. . . . Wash me, and I will be whiter than snow. (Psalm 51:1-3, 7)

TAKEAWAY

"I don't see how God can forgive me for what I have done." A Georgia prison chaplain says he has heard that statement over and over from inmates, some of whom have committed heinous crimes. His response is always, "Did you know that God is the God of the second chance? Did you know that when you confess your sins and determine to do them no more, he wipes the slate clean? Clean! You can make a new start!" The prerequisites are: (1) Ask God to forgive you, and mean it when you say, "I'm sorry." (2) Ask the people you have hurt to forgive you. (3) Tell God, "Never again."

Mind-Renewal Thought

Prayer for Forgiveness

Remove the stain of my guilt. Create in me a clean heart, O God. Renew a right spirit within me. . . . Make me willing to obey you.

PSALM 51:9-10, 12

Thinking It Over

No sin is too big to be thrown into His ocean of forgiveness.

—Dr. Bill Bright (1921–)

TAKEAWAY

Where is the foolish person who would think it in his power to commit more sins than God could forgive? And who will dare to measure, by the greatness of his crimes, the immensity of that infinite mercy which casts them all into the depths of the sea of oblivion, when we repent of them with love?

—St. Francis de Sales (1567–1622)

Day three

Mind-Renewal Thought

Could Your Sin Be Worse than Paul's?

I used to scoff at the name of Christ. I hunted down his people, harming them in every way I could. But God had mercy on me. . . . This is a true saying, and everyone should believe it: Christ Jesus came into the world to save sinners— and I was the worst of them all.

1 TIMOTHY 1:13, 15

Thinking It Over

Yes, it is true that the devastation and consequences of sin may hang around a long time, maybe forever (consider the reformed drunk driver who in the past ran over a child). A man who has come to God and made restitution for past mistakes may have to live with their consequences even though he knows that God has forgiven the sin itself. He may have to remind himself, "God has forgiven me—wiped the slate clean. And if he declares me white as snow because of Jesus' dying for me, then all is clear between me and my Creator." Isn't it an affront to God to go on holding past wrongdoings against ourselves when trying to make a fresh start? Would Paul?

TAKEAWAY

No matter what a man's past may have been, his future is spotless once he has taken the past to the Lord and claimed forgiveness.

—Anonymous

Day four

Mind-Renewal Thought

Brothers, listen! In this man Jesus there is forgiveness for your sins. Everyone who believes in him is freed from all guilt and declared right with God.

Acts 13:38-39

Thinking It Over

Sometimes I feel no release from past failures even though I have confessed and claimed the blood of Christ. When I continue at war with guilt, thinking my sin is the most awful on the planet, I will remind myself that every person sins. Everyone! Every man needs a savior. All of us have the potential for doing shameful things that destroy other people, even ourselves. I am no better, no worse. Now that I have come to Christ, I will not hold my past sins against myself. They are forgiven, and that is that! I will stand on the biblical fact of forgiveness, not on my feelings.

TAKEAWAY

For nothing good have I
Whereby Thy grace to claim—
I'll wash my garments white
In the blood of Calv'ry's Lamb.

—Elvina M. Hall (1820–1889)

Day five

Mind-Renewal Thought

For all have sinned; all fall short of God's glorious standard. Yet now God in his gracious kindness declares us not guilty. He has done this through Christ Jesus, who has freed us by taking away our sins.

ROMANS 3:23-24

Thinking It Over

How can God forgive you? The question is, "God loves you so much, how can he *not* forgive you?"

—Greg Johnson, *If I Could Ask God One Question*

TAKEAWAY

If guilt still overwhelms you after asking God's forgiveness, perhaps you need a mental shampoo that will help you confront the truth of your own forgiveness—words like this: "God of all forgiveness, *I* am forgiven! Yes, I *am* forgiven! I am *forgiven! I am forgiven!*"

Day. SIX

Mind-Renewal Thought

After Forgiveness, Then What?

[Jesus speaking:] Go and sin no more.

JOHN 8:11

Thinking It Over

David, too, sinned miserably (remember Bathsheba?). It started with adultery but led to lying and murder, all to cover up his first mistake. Yet God forgave and restored him, and he is cited as a man of faith (Hebrews 11:32), a man after God's own heart. After you have asked for forgiveness and turned to God, trust God to restore you.

TAKEAWAY

Satan will accuse us of badness that is already covered by Christ's blood. It is one of his best tricks to keep past sin before us. When guilt returns after confessing wrongdoing to God, and when I receive a message from Satan that says, "Surely God could not forget *that* sin," or "You have no right to feel free or to enjoy life because you have hurt someone deeply," I reply: "Buzz off, Satan." I cannot experience peace as long as I keep on hassling God about whether or not he has completely forgiven me.

—An anonymous Christian

Day seven

Mind-Renewal Thought

I Sinned Again Today! Now What?

My dear children, I am writing this to you so that you will not sin. But if you do sin, there is someone to plead for you before the Father. He is Jesus Christ, the one who pleases God completely. He is the sacrifice for our sins.

1 JOHN 2:1-2

Thinking It Over

When you go to God to ask forgiveness and you breathe out the sin to him, don't forget (and this is important) to breathe in the fresh air of forgiveness before going on your way! That is a very important part of the abundant life.

TAKEAWAY

What can wash away my sin?
Nothing but the blood of Jesus;
What can make me whole again?
Nothing but the blood of Jesus.

Oh! Precious is the flow
That makes me white as snow;
No other fount I know,
Nothing but the blood of Jesus.

—Robert Lowry (1826–1899)

POWERTHOUGHT

The Other Side of the Coin

There are some people who seem to take their repentance too lightly. For them, confession is like putting a coin into a candy machine—in goes the coin, out come delicious sweets, just a simple transaction. Forgiveness is serious business. It cost one sinless man terrible pain and suffering, so we had better mean business when we come before God, the creator of the universe, asking vindication of wrongs.

how's your love life?

Day one

Mind-Renewal Thought

Man Was Made to Love

If I could speak in any language in heaven or on earth but didn't love others, I would only be making meaningless noise like a loud gong or a clanging cymbal. If I had the gift of prophecy, and if I knew all the mysteries of the future and knew everything about everything, but didn't love others, what good would I be? And if I had the gift of faith so that I could speak to a mountain and make it move, without love I would be no good to anybody.

1 CORINTHIANS 13:1-2

Thinking It Over

Nine times out of ten when people say "love," they mean something else. They might be expressing the highly emotional state of "falling in love," which sees love simply as an overwhelming feeling. They might be confusing love with the selfish physical desire of lust. But they seldom have in mind the kind of selfless, courageous, and forgiving love Paul describes.

—*The Touchpoint Bible*

TAKEAWAY

Love is the key to the entire therapeutic program of the modern psychiatric hospital.

—Dr. Karl A. Menninger (1893–1990)

Mind-Renewal Thought

How Does Your Love Life Compare to This?

Love is patient and kind. Love is not jealous or boastful or proud or rude. Love does not demand its own way. Love is not irritable, and it keeps no record of when it has been wronged. It is never glad about injustice but rejoices whenever the truth wins out. Love never gives up, never loses faith, is always hopeful, and endures through every circumstance. Love will last forever.

1 CORINTHIANS 13:4-8

Thinking It Over

The plain truth is this: Love is not a matter of getting what you want. Quite the contrary. The insistence on always having what you want, on always being satisfied, on always being fulfilled, makes love impossible. Love is not a deal. It is a sacrifice.

—Thomas Merton (1915–1968)

TAKEAWAY

Do you dare take this test to see how much you really love? Read through Paul's words defining what love *really* is in 1 Corinthians 13:1-13. Now, substituting your own name for the words *I* and *we,* read the chapter again. How's *your* love life?

Mind-Renewal Thought

What's the Most Important Thing in Life?

[Jesus speaking] "The most important commandment is this: . . . 'The Lord our God is the one and only Lord. And you must love the Lord your God with all your heart, all your soul, all your mind, and all your strength.' The second is equally important: 'Love your neighbor as yourself.' No other commandment is greater than these."

MARK 12:29-31

Thinking It Over

We need to be loved and we need to give love. When we are thwarted in this, we suffer terribly.

—G. H. Montgomery

TAKEAWAY

Love for the Lord is not an ethereal, intellectual, dreamlike thing; it is the intensest, the most vital, the most passionate love of which the human heart is capable.

—Oswald Chambers (1874–1917)

Mind-Renewal Thought

Loving Others

God has called us to be holy. . . . Love one another. . . .
Love . . . more and more.

1 THESSALONIANS 4:7, 9-10

Thinking It Over

Only people who know God know what love is. It is an attitude of benevolence which is determined never to wish or seek anything but what is best for the other person, regardless of how that person acts, no matter how recklessly he hurts you or others. True Christian character is revealed in its love for the unlovely.

TAKEAWAY

A man's love for God can be measured by the love he has for the man he loves the least.

—Anonymous

Mind-Renewal Thought

Calvary: The True School of Love

Follow in his steps. He never sinned, and he never deceived anyone. He did not retaliate when he was insulted. When he suffered, he did not threaten to get even. He left his case in the hands of God, who always judges fairly. He personally carried away our sins in his own body on the cross. . . . You have been healed by his wounds!

1 PETER 2:21-24

Thinking It Over

God's love for me—it is the only constant remaining in this shifting, changing, and unsteady world that whirls menacingly around me faster than I can sometimes handle. That constant, relentless love pursues me forever, never stopping, never wavering, no matter what is going on in my life. That is my stability, my firm foundation. That is my peace. I will live within that love. As St. Augustine said, "God loves each of us as if there were only one of us."

TAKEAWAY

Loved with everlasting love,
Led by grace that love to know;
Spirit, breathing from above,
Thou hast taught me it is so!
Oh, this full and perfect peace!
Oh, this transport all divine!
In a love which cannot cease,
I am His, and He is mine.

—George W. Robinson (1838–1877)

Day. SIX

Mind-Renewal Thought

Lord, I Love You

The thing I seek most—is to live in the house of the Lord all the days of my life, delighting in the Lord's perfections and meditating in his Temple.

PSALM 27:4

Thinking It Over

Day by day, dear Lord,
Of Thee three things I pray:
To see Thee more clearly,
Love Thee more dearly,
Follow Thee more nearly,
Day by day.

—Richard of Chichester (1198–1253)

TAKEAWAY

Tell God now—aloud three times—"I love you, Lord." Now tell him why.

Mind-Renewal Thought

What's the use of saying you have faith if you don't prove it by your actions?

JAMES 2:14

Thinking It Over

Love takes many forms and most require some small or large sacrifice or giving up of rights. True Christians will show love just like their mentor, Christ. Here are unique ways others have put love into action:

When I was in my teens, my quiet and loving Dad, who had never even spanked me before, held a leather belt over me and said, "Go to your room and bring out the marijuana." Scared, I finally did it. Then he said, "If I ever catch you with drugs again, this belt will be laid on. I love you too much to stand by and watch you destroy yourself." I am thankful he did that for me. He risked my hating him (which I did) for quite a long time afterward. But I never experimented with drugs again.

With the help of God, I have learned that never, never saying, "I told you so," even when I want desperately to do it and it may be absolutely true, is not loving someone else. The next lesson: If you are wrong, say so. If you are right, just keep quiet and let the Lord show that to the other person.

One pastor-dad sobbed for an hour upon learning that his beloved daughter had been betrayed by a husband who ran off with two other women and even fathered two children. That is not at all what he had planned for his precious child when he married them on their wedding day. Yet, he began to pray for that adulterous man who had so hurt both his child and himself. "Perhaps some day I will pray him into the kingdom," said the father.

One husband said, "I have noticed that love flows back and softens my own heart, even when it's not reciprocated. When my pride has been hurt terribly by things said during an argument with my wife, I've learned to go by myself to cool off instead of yelling. Giving the silent treatment never works. A later touch on her shoulder or a weak smile, even when I don't at all feel like smiling, works better to soothe damaged pride and resentful feelings. Love is never lost."

TAKEAWAY

Human love fails and will always fail. God's love never fails.

—Corrie ten Boom (1892–1983)

POWERTHOUGHT

O Divine Master,
Grant that I may not so much seek
To be consoled, as to console;
To be understood as to understand;
To be loved as to love;
For it is in giving that we receive;
It is in pardoning that we are pardoned;
It is in dying that we are born to eternal life.

—St. Francis of Assisi (1182–1226)

for men who feel burned out

Day one

Mind-Renewal Thought

I will relieve your shoulder of its burden;
I will free your hands from their heavy tasks. . . .
But oh, that my people would listen to me!
PSALM 81:6, 13

Thinking It Over

In our weariness, God promises to refresh us when we turn to him. But do we? No, instead we poor overworked and overwhelmed human beings tire ourselves out by spending time mulling over our state of affairs and trying to remedy our problems on our own. How exhausting! What God really wants is for us to spend time in quiet meditation, asking *him* for answers, for *his* way out of a dilemma. Only our heavenly Father can see ahead. Only he has tomorrow in his hands! He is the one who can sustain, strengthen, and free us from unnecessary burdens. Only he knows what is best for his children. Surely with his tremendous power (didn't he rise from the dead?) and the unending love he has for us, he is more than able to instill in our human minds some answers that will open the way through the tiring times of debilitating fatigue. God relieves our burdens in ways we never would have thought of. Wait in prayer then, trust and watch him work!

TAKEAWAY

I will focus on God's incredible power to heal and help. I will assume he has a solution to these intense feelings of burnout, and I will wait for him to act. Whatever the outcome, I leave it to my heavenly Father who loved me enough to give his life for me and knows what is best for me.

Mind-Renewal Thought

Need A Break? Try Sunday. It Was God's Idea

Remember to observe the Sabbath day by keeping it holy. Six days a week are set apart for your daily duties and regular work, but the seventh day is a day of rest dedicated to the Lord your God. . . . The Lord blessed the Sabbath day and set it apart as holy.

EXODUS 20:8-11

Thinking It Over

Finding Rest

The Sabbath is a good gift. When was the last time you set aside time to take a hike in the woods with the family? read a novel? peruse the Bible's depths or memorize some of it? take a real look into a rose to appreciate its unbelievable beauty? count the rings in a tree stump? lounge in the hammock watching the clouds drift by? Maybe this very weekend you can purposely take God's suggestion for a Sunday break.

TAKEAWAY

Take rest; a field that has rested gives a bountiful crop.

—Ovid (43 B.C.–A.D. 17)

Day three

Mind-Renewal Thought

Give your burdens to the Lord, and he will take care of you.

Psalm 55:22

Thinking It Over

Remember Moses? He had enough stress to cause major burnout trying to guide unruly and rebellious Israelites to the Promised Land. Surely his task seemed insurmountable when he viewed the wide expanse of the Red Sea and knew that his life and the lives of thousands of others depended on his getting them safely across. No boats available! Pharaoh's army hard at his heels! But the Lord had given Moses the assignment, so Moses led out across the sea by faith that his heavenly Father knew what he was doing when he asked Moses to move ahead and trust. It was to be the Lord's battle, not his. The sea parted to let them through on dry land! But Pharaoh's army was drowned by the waves. God hasn't changed. The same God who delivered Moses in extreme conditions, under tremendous pressure, is still available to his stressed-out people today if they trust him as they move ahead. "I am the Lord, and I do not change" (Malachi 3:6).

TAKEAWAY

Day by day and with each passing moment,
Strength I find to meet my trials here;
Trusting in my Father's wise bestowment,
I've no cause for worry or for fear.
He whose heart is kind beyond all measure
Gives unto each day what he deems best—
Lovingly, its part of pain and pleasure,
Mingling toil with peace and rest.

—Carolina Sandell Berg (1832–1903)

Mind-Renewal Thought

Be still in the presence of the Lord, and wait patiently for him to act.

PSALM 37:7

Thinking It Over

Perhaps your burnout is a result of busyness that pushed time alone with God out of your life entirely or cut it back. Sometimes prayer life becomes rote, a burden, a daily requirement, rather than a time of refreshment. One overworked businessman said, "When I'm exhausted, I can't wait to get away from the world. Rest begins when I hear the sound of the den door closing quietly behind me in the sure knowledge that I will be alone to talk, undisturbed, with God, creator of the universe, my loving heavenly Father. It is there that I get to see how great he is, how much of my weariness he understands, and his great power to help; and especially I am reminded that it is he who is in control of things, not me."

TAKEAWAY

To Help You Regain Peace of Mind

An inner sense of wholeness and peace is what you are after. Make a plan to get up early for an expanded prayer-quiet time for two weeks as part of your healing from burnout. Read Bible passages like these that remind you who your Helper is and what he is like:

> *God is my helper. He is a friend of mine!* (Psalm 54:4, TLB)
>
> *Don't you know that the Lord is the everlasting God, the Creator of all the earth? He never grows faint or weary. No one can measure the depths of his understanding. He gives power to those who are tired and worn out; he offers strength to the weak. Even youths will become*

> exhausted, and young men will give up. But those who wait on the Lord will find new strength. They will fly high on wings like eagles. They will run and not grow weary. They will walk and not faint. (Isaiah 40:28-31)

Pray Bible prayers like these: Psalm 23; 70:1, 4-5; 131:1-2; 148:7-13; Lamentations 3:22-26.

Each day, sing, or read aloud the words to this or other quieting hymns three times:

Breathe through the heats of our [my] desire
Thy coolness and thy balm;
Let sense be dumb, let flesh retire,
Speak through the earthquake, wind, and fire
O still small voice of calm!

—John Greenleaf Whittier (1807–1892)

Mind-Renewal Thought

There is a time for everything, a season for every activity under heaven. . . . A time to cry and a time to laugh. A time to grieve and a time to dance.

ECCLESIASTES 3:1, 4

Thinking It Over

Your mental health will be better if you have lots of fun outside of that office.

—William Menninger

How to Conquer Feelings of Exhaustion

Practice lifting your mind above the confusion and irritation around you. Form mental pictures of the great hills and mountain ranges, or the wide sweep of the ocean, or of some great valley spreading out before you. Get a mental picture of the stars serene in the heavens, or of the moon sailing high on a clean, calm night. Hang these pictures on the walls of your mind and think about them habitually. One can do this while busy on a job.

—Dr. Norman Vincent Peale (1898–1993)

Day.
SIX

Mind-Renewal Thought

Cease striving and know that I am God.

PSALM 46:10, NASB

Thinking It Over

We return to You, O Lord, that our souls may rise from their weariness toward You. With You is refreshment and true strength.

—St. Augustine (354–430)

TAKEAWAY

Someone has said, "For peace of mind, resign as general manager of the universe." Professional counselors generally agree that the root cause of tension and resulting burnout is too much worry about how you are doing or a frantic sense of competition with other people. The remedy? Don't try to do things perfectly, but do the best you can, and compete primarily with yourself.

Mind-Renewal Thought

You anoint my head with oil.

PSALM 23:5, NIV

Thinking It Over

God sometimes has trouble arresting our attention; amidst all the distractions, we aren't even aware of his presence. Right now, be still, and envision God laying hands gently on your head, his healing power of quietness pouring into you, his love overpowering you: I lay My Loving Hands on you in blessing. Wait in love and longing to feel their tender pressure and, as you wait, courage and hope will flow into your being, irradiating your life with the warm sun of My Presence. Let all go. Loosen your hold on earth, its care, its worries, even its joys.

Unclasp your hands, relax and the tide of joy will come.

—A. J. Russell

TAKEAWAY

When I am with God,
My fear is gone
In the great quiet of God.
My troubles are as the pebbles on the road,
My joys are like the everlasting hills.

—Walter Rauschenbusch (1861–1918)

POWERTHOUGHT

Finish every day and be done with it. You have done what you could. Some blunders and absurdities no doubt crept in; forget them as soon as you can. Tomorrow is a new day; begin it well and serenely and with too high a spirit to be cumbered with your old nonsense. This day is all that is good and fair. It is too dear, with its hopes and invitations, to waste a moment on the yesterdays.

—Ralph Waldo Emerson (1803–1882)

men, women, marriage, and sexuality

Mind-Renewal Thought

Woman—God's Provision for Men's Lifetime Companionship

The Lord God said, "It is not good for the man to be alone. I will make a companion who will help him." . . . So the Lord God caused Adam to fall into a deep sleep. He took one of Adam's ribs and closed up the place from which he had taken it. Then the Lord God made a woman from the rib and brought her to Adam. "At last!" Adam exclaimed. "She is part of my own flesh and bone!"

GENESIS 2:18, 21-23

Thinking It Over

When Adam first saw Eve he shouted something like, "This is it!" Was he excited! And so he should have been. She was outstanding, and God had made her especially for him. Neither Adam nor Eve could "multiply and fill the earth" by themselves. They were made for each other and they needed each other. And so this uniquely created man and woman began to explore the wonders of their God-ordained intimacy with excitement and delight. Many marriages lack this sense of adventure and exploration, even though they, too, are uniquely created and ordained by God. But men would regain some of this excitement if they would view their wives as Adam viewed Eve. If the modern Adam would recognize his Eve as a divine piece of work, marriages would be immeasurably transformed. Viewed like this, any husband, as he looks at his wife, should not have too much difficulty exclaiming, "Wow, she's outstanding, and God has entrusted her to me!"

—*Daily Study Bible for Men*

TAKEAWAY

O perfect Love, all human thought transcending,
Lowly we kneel in prayer before Thy throne,
That theirs may be the love which knows no ending,
Whom Thou forevermore dost join in one.

—Dorothy Frances Blomfield Gurney (1858–1932)

Mind-Renewal Thought

Permanency of the Marriage Union

Since they are no longer two but one, let no one separate them, for God has joined them together.

MATTHEW 19:6

Thinking It Over

Remember the wedding vow? "To have and to hold from this day forward, for better, for worse, for richer, for poorer, in sickness and in health, to love and to cherish, till death do us part." It's our responsibility to follow through with our wedding vow. God's Word says: "Once you have voluntarily made a vow, be careful to do as you have said, for you have made a vow to the Lord your God" (Deuteronomy 23:23).

TAKEAWAY

To keep a vow, therefore, means not to keep from breaking it, but rather to devote the rest of one's life discovering what the vow means, and to be willing to change and to grow accordingly.

—Mike Mason

Day three

Mind-Renewal Thought

Sex—God's Gift to Couples

Kiss me again and again, for your love is sweeter than wine. . . . Bring me into your bedroom. . . . Oh, how delightful you are, my beloved; how pleasant for utter delight!

SONG OF SONGS 1:2, 4; 7:6

Thinking It Over

The sex relationship offers no more cherished pleasure than this *knowing* of the one you love. With the understanding that our marriage relationship portrays the truths of our relationship with God, we can become free as never before to express our love for our husband or wife fully through the dynamic opportunity of the sex act.

—Ed Wheat

TAKEAWAY

Love is an image of God, and not a lifeless image, but the living essence of the divine nature which beams full of all goodness.

—Martin Luther (1483–1546)

Mind-Renewal Thought

Words to Husbands

Who can find a virtuous and capable wife? She is worth more than precious rubies. Her husband can trust her, and she will greatly enrich his life.

PROVERBS 31:10-11

Thinking It Over

As the husband is, the wife is.

—Alfred, Lord Tennyson (1809–1892)

TAKEAWAY

We are quite right in saying that marriage is based on love; we find this truth in the Gospel. However, we must immediately add that true love makes us capable of taking on the tasks and problems of married and family life and that if it does not give us this capacity it cannot be called love. (Love endures through every circumstance. 1 Corinthians 13:7)

—Pope John Paul II

Day five

Mind-Renewal Thought

All about Adultery

Give honor to marriage, and remain faithful to one another in marriage. God will surely judge people who are immoral and those who commit adultery.

HEBREWS 13:4

Thinking It Over

O that such may be our union,
As thine with the Father is,
And not one of our communion
E'er forsake the path of bliss;
May our light 'fore men with brightness,
From thy light reflected shine;
Thus the world will bear us witness,
That we, Lord, are truly thine.

—Count Nikolaus L. von Zinzendorf (1700–1760)

TAKEAWAY

What begins as a series of seemingly small indiscretions [in an opposite-sex friendship] can add up to major traps. Maybe at first it seems innocent and safe, but then you say or do something you never thought you'd say or do. That's why we all need "hedges"—precautions that we have planned out ahead of time and we adhere to in order to protect our marriages. These hedges can provide a way to avoid potentially dangerous relationships before they get started. For the benefit of every marriage, we all need to set our own ground rules. And then stick to them.

—Jerry B. Jenkins

Day.
SIX

Mind-Renewal Thought

Husbands ought to love their wives as they love their own bodies. For a man is actually loving himself when he loves his wife.

EPHESIANS 5:28

Thinking It Over

The nearer you keep to Christ, the nearer you will be to one another.

—Geoffrey Francis Fisher, archbishop of Canterbury, at the wedding of Princess Elizabeth

TAKEAWAY

God-Style Love between a Man and Woman

When it comes to interaction with your wife, it can be challenging to use biblical principles to respond. But the Bible is very clear about how you are to interact with your wife. Look up the following verses, and use them as guidelines for your relationship: Proverbs 31:31; 1 Thessalonians 5:11; James 1:26; 5:16; 1 Peter 3:7-9.

Ask God to bring them to mind so that you can interact in the ways he intends.

Day
seven

Mind-Renewal Thought

The Bible Speaks on Homosexuality

Those who indulge in sexual sin, who are idol worshipers, adulterers, male prostitutes, homosexuals, thieves, greedy people, drunkards, abusers, and swindlers—none of these will have a share in the Kingdom of God. . . . Our bodies were not made for sexual immorality. They were made for the Lord, and the Lord cares about our bodies.

1 CORINTHIANS 6:9-10, 13

Thinking It Over

There has never yet been a bomb invented that is half so powerful as one mortal sin—and yet there is no positive power in sin, only negation, only annihilation.

—Thomas Merton (1915–1968)

TAKEAWAY

Some men make wrong choices when it comes to love. The Bible makes it clear that homosexuality and all other sexual sins are offensive to God. Many gay men have expressed a desire to leave their lifestyle but do not know that there are counselors and books available to help. For more information, contact Focus on the Family, Box 35500, Colorado Springs, CO 80995. Here are some helpful books:

Love Won Out by John and Anne Paulk

Hope for the Homosexual by Jeffrey Satinover, M.D.

Coming Out of Homosexuality by Bob Davies and Lori Rentzel

POWERTHOUGHT

God, who invented marriage, who laid out a plan for couples, and who sets a high premium on keeping his pledges, must surely hate what he sees today—divorce, living together without marriage, spousal abuse, perverted sex, couples arguing before a judge about money or children. He who himself is the epitome of faithfulness, sees broken vows everywhere among his beloved children. He must be heartbroken, sorely grieved: "You cover the Lord's altar with tears, weeping and groaning because he pays no attention. . . . You cry out, 'Why has the Lord abandoned us?' I'll tell you why! Because the Lord witnessed the vows you and your wife made to each other on your wedding day when you were young. But you have been disloyal to her, though she remained your faithful companion, the wife of your marriage vows."

MALACHI 2:13-14

the single man

Day one

Mind-Renewal Thought

Paul's View of Singleness

I am saying this . . . not to place restrictions on you. I want you to do whatever will help you serve the Lord best, with as few distractions as possible. But if a man thinks he ought to marry . . . it is all right. . . . But if he has decided firmly not to marry and there is no urgency and he can control his passion, he does well not to marry. So the person who marries does well, and the person who doesn't marry does even better.

1 Corinthians 7:35-38

Thinking It Over

"Father . . . may your will be done" (Matthew 6:9-10). Some men choose the single life and find it fulfilling. Jesus remained single by choice throughout his thirty-three years. He knew he could focus more intensely on doing his Father's work. Others, like the widowed, divorced, or abandoned, have tasted some of the joys (and sorrows) of marriage but now must live single by circumstance. Some men postpone the commitments of matrimony when they apprehensively look around to see that about half of all marriages end in divorce. Whether single by choice or circumstance, it is important to make the best of things and to take care not to become self-centered or to shrivel up into self-pity.

TAKEAWAY

The happiest people don't necessarily have the best of everything. They just make the best of everything.

—Roy O. Disney

Mind-Renewal Thought

The Source of Contentment

I have learned to be content whatever the circumstances. . . . I have learned the secret of being content in any and every situation. . . . I can do everything through him who gives me strength.

PHILIPPIANS 4:11-13, NIV

Thinking It over

People, places, and things were never meant to give us life. God alone is the author of a fulfilling life.

—Arnold Glasgow

TAKEAWAY

Assignment for today: If you are single, do not succumb to the feeling that your life is incomplete without a partner. Ask God to show you how to use your gifts, including your single status, to serve him and find fulfillment. "You are complete through your union with Christ" (Colossians 2:10).

Mind-Renewal Thought

The Privilege of Being Single

In everything you do, I want you to be free from the concerns of this life. An unmarried man can spend his time doing the Lord's work and thinking how to please him. But a married man can't do that so well. He has to think about his earthly responsibilities and how to please his wife. His interests are divided.

1 CORINTHIANS 7:32-34

Thinking It Over

Either marriage or singleness can be a gift from God. There are advantages to both. One widower said, "I do not wish to marry again even though I had a wonderful wife and a happy first marriage. I simply have gotten used to living alone and would find it too difficult to once more adjust to another's different or perhaps difficult habits, time schedules, eating preferences, and small quirks. Sometimes loneliness sets in, but I have friends and a Friend, and I have learned to keep busy by volunteering extra hours at a local museum."

TAKEAWAY

We live overflowing lives because the *Source* of life, instead of the *gifts* (people, places, possessions, and position) of life, brings us contentment. How? By leading us to the well that never runs dry.

—Gary and Norma Smalley

Day four

Mind-Renewal Thought

Looking for Love

Don't team up with those who are unbelievers. How can goodness be a partner with wickedness? How can light live with darkness? . . . How can a believer be a partner with an unbeliever? . . . For we are the temple of the living God. As God said: "I will live in them and walk among them. I will be their God, and they will be my people. Therefore, come out from them and separate yourselves from them."

2 CORINTHIANS 6:14-17

Thinking It Over

Consider what happened to Solomon (presumably the world's wisest man), who decided to ignore the advice of God's law, which clearly told him not to marry women of other faiths. Sure enough, in later years these wives turned

Solomon's heart to worshiping *their* gods instead of trusting only in the Lord his God. Those who marry in haste often regret at leisure. When looking for love, biographical or educational facts are of little help. It is commitment to Christ and character that count. Experts say that marrying someone with the same values matters greatly.

TAKEAWAY

What an absurdity is it to think of joining righteousness and unrighteousness, or mingling light and darkness, fire and water, together! Believers are, and should be, righteous; but unbelievers are unrighteous. Believers are made light in the Lord, but unbelievers are in darkness; and what comfortable communion can these have together?

—Matthew Henry (1662–1714)

Day five

Mind-Renewal Thought

Tempted by Sex

The lips of an immoral woman are as sweet as honey, and her mouth is smoother than oil. But the result is as bitter as poison, sharp as a double-edged sword. Her feet go down to death; her steps lead straight to the grave. For she does not care about the path to life. She staggers down a crooked trail and doesn't even realize where it leads. So now, my sons, listen to me. Never stray from what I am about to say: Run from her! Don't go near the door of her house! If you do, you will lose your honor and hand over to merciless people everything you have achieved in life. Strangers will obtain your wealth, and someone else will enjoy the fruit of your labor. Afterward you will groan in anguish when disease consumes your body, and you will say, "How I hated discipline! If only I had not demanded my own way! Oh, why didn't I listen to my teachers? Why didn't I pay attention to those who gave me instruction? . . . Now I must face public disgrace."

PROVERBS 5:3-14

Thinking It Over

O for a faith that will not shrink,
Though pressed by many a foe,
That will not tremble on the brink
Of any earthly woe.

—William H. Bathurst (1796–1877)

TAKEAWAY

Take love when love is given. But never think to find it a sure escape from sorrow, or a complete repose.

—Sara Teasdale (1884–1933)

Mind-Renewal Thought

My Heavenly Companion

If you give yourself to the Lord, you and Christ are joined together as one person.

1 CORINTHIANS 6:17, TLB

Thinking It Over

When we have nothing left but God, then we become aware that God is enough.

—M. Rowden

TAKEAWAY

Dr. Allan Fromme gives these bits of advice for people who want to help themselves through loneliness:

Keep moving. Let no week go by without giving

or accepting an invitation. If no one calls you, call someone.

Practice speaking to new people. If necessary, learn lines in advance: what to say at parties, buffet suppers, etc.

Remember, the easiest social skill, and the most endearing, is to know how to listen.

Find every possible way to be with people, to do things with people, to become involved with people.

Day seven

Mind-Renewal Thought

Wise Words for Singles to Consider

Let us run with patience the particular race that God has set before us. Keep your eyes on Jesus, our leader and instructor.

HEBREWS 12:1-2, TLB

Thinking It Over

One was never married, and that's his hell; another is, and that's his plague.

—Robert Burton (1577–1640)

TAKEAWAY

A man is only as good as what (or who) he loves.

—Saul Bellow

POWERTHOUGHT

There is little doubt that all men, married or single, should nurture and develop singleness of vision for a lost world. Every believing man should be ready to heed the Savior's words, "Look around you! Vast fields are ripening all around us and are ready now for the harvest" (John 4:35). The single man does not have to balance family and ministry, so he should not have any problem being devoted to the Lord and his work. Yet many single men are totally devoted to their own personal concerns. They, like many others, lack the necessary vision. But, singleness is an aid to single-mindedness, to keeping focus. The single person should be encouraged to identify and exercise his spiritual gifts for the benefit of the church and the glory of God. One of the great blessings for single people exercising their gifts for the good of the body and the glory of God is that many singles begin to discover through their ministry a new significance and a great boost to their drooping spirits. There is no such thing as an insignificant member of the body of Christ.

—Daily Study Bible for Men

help for men who want to overcome a bad habit

Day one

Mind-Renewal Thought

Encourage me by your word. Keep me from lying to myself.

PSALM 119:28-29

Thinking It Over

We have followed too much the devices and desires of our own hearts. We have offended against Thy holy laws. We have left undone those things which we ought to have done; and we have done those things which we ought not to have done; and there is no health in us. But Thou, O Lord, have mercy upon us, miserable offenders.

—*The Book of Common Worship*

TAKEAWAY

Being honest about our sin is difficult. We try to convince ourselves that we are just fine: "I'm not that bad. Look at what Joe did at work. I've never done that." Or, "I would never cheat on my wife—so what if I told her a little lie about where I was." Yet God calls us to his standard, and we must bring our hearts to him for examination. As the Scripture says:

> *Put to death the sinful, earthly things lurking within you. Have nothing to do with sexual sin, impurity, lust, and shameful desires. Don't be greedy for the good things of this life, for that is idolatry. God's terrible anger will come upon those who do such things. . . . Now is the time to get rid of anger, rage, malicious behavior, slander, and dirty language. Don't lie to each other, for you have stripped off your old evil nature and all its wicked deeds.* (Colossians 3:5-6, 8-9)

Assignment: Consider other habits that may need fixing by reading Romans 1:27-32 and the Ten Commandments in Exodus 20:1-17.

Day two

Mind-Renewal Thought

Temptation comes from the lure of our own evil desires. These evil desires lead to evil actions.

JAMES 1:14-15

Thinking It Over

When men are dealing with bad habits, becoming aware of the awesomeness and holiness of God helps them want to change. In Isaiah 6, Isaiah catches a glimpse of his glorious and powerful Creator amidst a mighty chorus of angels singing praises: "Holy, holy, holy is the Lord Almighty!" (v. 3). The singing shook the temple and filled it with smoke. Seeing the magnificent and powerful God changed Isaiah forever, so he was able to humble himself before God and cry out, "I am a sinful man and a member of a sinful race. Yet I have seen the

King, the Lord Almighty!" (v. 5) He confessed his own unholiness then and there! Wouldn't you? Taking a good look at the reality of God's holiness, the thinking man cannot help but realize how far short he is of God's magnificent perfection. Humbling himself, he will acknowledge and desire to change his behavior so that it matches biblical commandments given by a loving heavenly Father, who wants only the best for his children. Here is where it all starts for today's man who wants to unload ingrained habits.

TAKEAWAY

We are creatures of habit. Most of what men know is learned by doing the same things over and over. Good men unwittingly or willfully build up years of hurtful habits this way. More often than not, these were learned as young boys, many simply following what Dad did. Father-son conduct then seems normal, not deviant, and when confronted, men will often build a defensive shell around themselves, denying their actions are hurtful. They see themselves as masters of their own lives, people who really don't need a lot of modification. Many a good man has trouble admitting decades of wrong actions. The man who denies chooses the same sort of behavior over and over until it entraps like a cable, built thread by thread, almost impossible to break. It is God who created us. He is every Christian man's owner. He knows what is the best way to live and has written it down in Scripture. A Christian who has willingly sold himself to be God's man here on Earth trusts the rules for life his Leader outlined in the manual. . . . Realizing the holiness and perfection of God has humbled me and given me an inner core that desires to please him—that would rather not be in bondage to harmful habits. That is my motivation to change.

—A New York pastor and counselor

Day three

Mind-Renewal Thought

You Are Not Alone Wrestling with a Habit You Wish to Break

[Paul speaking] I don't understand myself at all, for I really want to do what is right, but I don't do it. Instead, I do the very thing I hate. I know perfectly well that what I am doing is wrong, and my bad conscience shows that I agree that the law is good. But I can't help myself, because it is sin inside me that makes me do these evil things. . . . No matter which way I turn, I can't make myself do right. I want to, but I can't. When I want to do good, I don't. And when I try not to do wrong, I do it anyway. . . . I love God's law with all my heart. But there is another law at work within me that is at war with my mind. . . . Oh, what a miserable person I am! Who will free me from this life that is dominated by sin? [The answer to Paul's question] Thank God! The answer is in Jesus Christ our Lord.

ROMANS 7:15-25

Thinking It Over

Willpower does not change men. Time does not change men. Christ does. We must go to the source and change the inmost nature, and the angry humors will die away of themselves. Souls are made sweet not by taking the acid fluids out but by putting something in—a great love, a new spirit, the Spirit of Christ.

—Henry Drummond (1851–1897), *The Greatest Thing in the World*

Fire tries iron, and temptation tries a just man.

—Thomas à Kempis (1380–1471)

Day four

Mind-Renewal Thought

[Jesus speaking] Keep alert and pray. Otherwise temptation will overpower you. For though the spirit is willing enough, the body is weak!

MATTHEW 26:41

Thinking It Over

Prayers Asking God's Help in Overcoming

One pastor's prayer: "Heavenly Father, you are my loving ally. Show me my sinful habits. Heal my waywardness, especially my hardness of heart and my defensiveness when I discover habits that need changing. I claim your strength to overcome my corrupt nature, especially when the pull of an old behavior pattern becomes strong. Being your son has made me want to live up to the family name. I want to worship you with all my being, with everything that is in me. I am willing to overcome. Right now I claim your immense power to help me turn aside. In Jesus' name, amen."

Scripture prayers for help: Psalms 19:12-13; 119:123-125; 141:3-4; 143:8, 10; Matthew 6:13.

When temptation knocks at the door, I ask Jesus to answer.

—Corrie ten Boom (1892–1983)

Day five

Mind-Renewal Thought

You Can Do It!

All power and authority are his. . . . He is able to keep you from slipping and falling away, and to bring you, sinless and perfect, into his glorious presence with mighty shouts of everlasting joy.

JUDE 1:24-25, TLB

Thinking It Over

Testimony from Someone Who Has Struggled with Bad Habits

The God I serve loves me very much. Apart from him, I am weak as water in overcoming. I am convinced that he is as close as breathing to help, and he knows my deep, deep desire for change. Time and time again, when the urge for the bad habit returns, when I reach a point where I am almost "into" the wrong behavior, God is faithful to remind me just *before* the gossip slips out, *before* I am critical of someone, *before* I reach for that next cigarette, or *before* I spout off in anger. Once in a while God reminds me in the middle of committing the offensive thing. Either way, when I stand at the cross-roads, I realize I have a choice—to pay attention to God's way or my own way. Often I choose to back off and remember the Scripture from Isaiah 30:21: "You will hear a voice say, 'This is the way; turn around and walk here.' "

—A Christian schoolteacher

TAKEAWAY

Temptations that find us dwelling in God are to our faith like winds that more firmly root the tree.

—Anonymous

Day.
SIX

Mind-Renewal Thought

How to Resist Repeating a Bad Habit

Be strong with the Lord's mighty power. Put on all of God's armor so that you will be able to stand firm against all strategies and tricks of the Devil. For we are not fighting against people made of flesh and blood, but against the evil rulers and authorities of the unseen world, against those mighty powers of darkness who rule this world. . . . Use every piece of God's armor to resist the enemy in the time of evil, so that after the battle you will still be standing firm. Stand your ground, putting on the sturdy belt of truth and the body armor of God's righteousness. For shoes, put on the peace that comes from the Good News, so that you will be fully prepared. In every battle you will need faith as your shield to stop the fiery arrows aimed at you by Satan. Put on salvation as your helmet, and take the sword of the Spirit, which is the word of God. Pray at all times and on every occasion . . . and be persistent in your prayers.

EPHESIANS 6:10-18

Thinking It Over

Satan's strategy is to keep God's people in bondage, sometimes by placing thoughts in their minds like "I'll change tomorrow." So we often push God away and find it easier to continue the old habits for a while longer. Caution from God's Word: "Come to terms quickly with your enemy" (Matthew 5:25). "Resist the Devil, and he will flee from you" (James 4:7).

TAKEAWAY

He who will fight the devil with his own weapons must not wonder if he finds him an overmatch.

—Robert South (1634–1716)

Day seven

Mind-Renewal Thought

The Flip Side

Thank you for making me so wonderfully complex!
Your workmanship is marvelous—
and how well I know it.

PSALM 139:14

Thinking It Over

Sometimes when I pray, I speak freely with the Master who smiles at me and encourages me when I do the right thing. This is the voice that says, "Well done, good and faithful servant."

Some days I think of myself as bowing before my Master, knowing in my heart that I have served as faithfully as I've understood how. Yet it's often difficult for me to hear the voice say, "Well done." I hear instead, "Ah, that's pride speaking. You're not humble if you think you deserve to hear the Master say you've done well. Even at best, you're still not good enough."

Yet God exhorts us to faithfulness. Only God knows whether or when we measure up. I like to think of God as a kind Master. By that I don't mean an old softie or someone to manipulate, but a God who smiles at me when I do the right thing; when I treat someone else the way I want to be treated; when I do a spontaneous act of kindness; when I sincerely listen to a troubled friend. In those instances, I don't think it's pride that allows me to hear the words "Well done." I'm enjoying a relationship in which I believe I often please God.

—Cecil Murphey

TAKEAWAY

List here a few good habits in your life right now—some things you like about yourself. Maybe some, like perseverance, happened as a result of your working hard to unload a bad one. It is important that a man not see himself as all bad just because some distressing habits still plague his life. From God's perspective, every Christian has some bad, but also a lot of good in him. God sees and respects our desire to do better. Shouldn't we?

POWERTHOUGHT

I never knew a man to overcome a bad habit gradually.

—John R. Mott (1865–1955)

for men who are too busy

Day one

Mind-Renewal Thought

It is useless for you to work so hard from early morning until late at night, anxiously working for food to eat; for God gives rest to his loved ones.

PSALM 127:2

Thinking It Over

Slow me down, Lord.
Ease the pounding of my heart by the quieting of my mind.
Steady my harried pace
With a vision of the eternal reach of time.
Give me, amidst the confusion of my day,
The calmness of the everlasting hills.
Break the tension of my nerves
With the soothing music of the singing streams
That live in my memory.
Help me to know the magical restoring power of sleep.

Teach me the art of taking minute vacations
of slowing down
To look at a flower;
To chat with an old friend or make a new one;
To pat a stray dog; to watch a spider build a web;
To smile at a child; or to read from a good book.
Remind me each day
That the race is not always to the swift;
That there is more to life than increasing its speed.
Let me look upward into the towering oak
And know that it grew great and strong
Because it grew slowly and well.
Slow me down, Lord,
And inspire me to send my roots deep
Into the soil of life's enduring values
That I may grow toward the stars of my greater
destiny.

—O. L. Crain

God loves an idle rainbow no less than laboring seas.

—Ralph Hodgson (1871–1962)

Day two

Mind-Renewal Thought

I have observed something in this world of ours. The fastest runner doesn't always win the race, and the strongest warrior doesn't always win the battle.

ECCLESIASTES 9:11

Thinking It Over

Busyness is a chief weapon of Satan. It keeps us from the immense power that comes with spending quiet time for thinking creatively, for reflecting, and for spending time with family, friends, and God. Perhaps a good way to deal with the hurry-up pace of this world is to do what Jesus did and respond to Satan's push with Scripture beginning with the words "It is written." One good verse to quote aloud when the enemy harasses us is Ecclesiastes 3:1: "There is a time for everything, a season for every activity under heaven." Pray this prayer: "Lord, make me accountable to you for my faithfulness in relaxing."

TAKEAWAY

The concern of modern life is not how to worship in catacombs but how to remain human in skyscrapers.

—Abraham J. Heschel (1907–1972)

Day three

Mind-Renewal Thought

Seventy years are given to us! Some may even reach eighty. . . . Teach us to make the most of our time.

PSALM 90:10, 12

Thinking It Over

We have what we seek. It is there all the time, and if we give it time, it will make itself known to us.

—Thomas Merton (1915–1968)

TAKEAWAY

One ought every day at least to hear a little song, read a good poem, see a fine picture, and if possible, to speak a few reasonable words.

—Johann Wolfgang von Goethe (1749–1832)

Mind-Renewal Thought

As pressure and stress bear down on me . . .
you are near, O Lord.

PSALM 119:143, 151

Thinking It Over

Hurried people, always in a rush, never have time to recover. When the frenzy of the workplace gets too much, the Lord waits for you to come to him. Quietness is your strength. In the midst of the turmoil, think about a place where you can go by yourself to pray just for a few minutes to regain your confidence. Pray this prayer: "When doubts fill my mind, when my heart is in turmoil, quiet me and give me renewed hope and cheer" (Psalm 94:19, TLB).

TAKEAWAY 

We mutter, we sputter,
We fume, and we spurt;
We mumble and grumble,
Our feelings get hurt;
We can't understand things,
Our vision grows dim;
When all that we need is
A moment with Him.

—*Discovery Digest*

Mind-Renewal Thought

Being too busy gives you nightmares.
ECCLESIASTES 5:3

Thinking It Over

People often ask me, "How do you maintain your spiritual high? What do you do on a day-to-day basis?" I tell them about my quiet time. Some days it is early, sometimes it is late. Without it, my Christian life would be a wilderness.

—Billy Graham (1918–)

TAKEAWAY

Oh, how great peace and quietness would he possess who should cut off all vain anxiety and place all his confidence in God.

—Thomas à Kempis (1380–1471)

Day. SIX

Mind-Renewal Prayer

"Lord, remind me how brief my time on earth will be. Remind me that my days are numbered, and that my life is fleeing away. My life is no longer than the width of my hand. An entire lifetime is just a moment to you; human existence is but a breath." We are merely moving shadows, and all our busy rushing ends in nothing. . . . And so, Lord, where do I put my hope? My only hope is in you.

PSALM 39:4-7

Thinking It Over

Is some of your busyness self-inflicted? In today's world we seem to have to be on the go—involved in restless activity, planning something, or mapping out our lives. Otherwise, we feel unproductive. Preoccupied with our own usefulness, we are an uneasy generation, sometimes mistaking activity for relationship. But such ambition often puts men in bondage. For the sake of making a living, we forget to live. We forget that time spent "receiving" life is just as important as giving or doing. Our priorities get out of kilter, and we forget to save time for tossing around a football with the kids, enjoying a romantic seaside picnic with the woman we love most, or delighting in an afternoon spent reading in a backyard hammock. Yet these are the very activities that refresh and revive us so we can keep the pace when 8 A.M. arrives on Monday morning. Are you allowing balance between work and time for yourself?

TAKEAWAY

To help you put your priorities in order, measure your wealth, not by the things you have, but by the things you have for which you would not take money. Then allot your time accordingly.

Day seven

Mind-Renewal Thought

[Jesus speaking] How do you benefit if you gain the whole world but lose your own soul in the process?

MATTHEW 16:26

Thinking It Over

Dr. Laura Schlessinger believes that families with two parents who work outside the home all day contribute to much of the busyness in the world as well as the neglect of their children's needs. She notes that in her counseling experience, a way can almost always be found so one parent can stay at home to give more time to the children and act as a backup to the other. Selfishness and yearning for material things seem to be the biggest drawback. Would it help your situation to cut back on buying, lower your standard of living a little, and allow your mate to quit a job? Think about it. God delights in watching his people enjoy the lives he gave them, and he works the night shift watching over his own.

TAKEAWAY

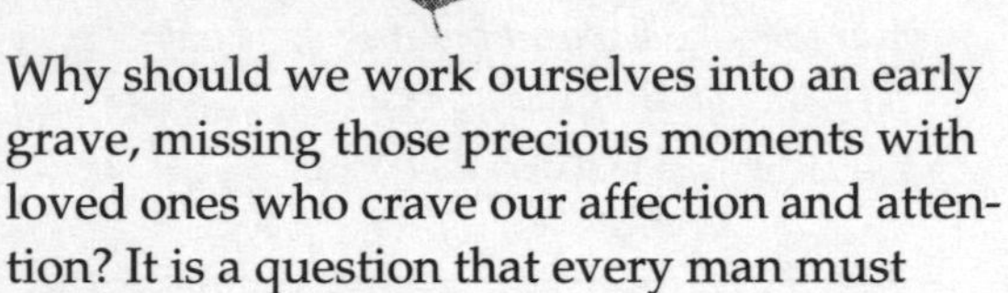

Why should we work ourselves into an early grave, missing those precious moments with loved ones who crave our affection and attention? It is a question that every man must consider.

—Dr. James C. Dobson (1936–)

POWERTHOUGHT

Which of us expects to say on our deathbed, "I wish I had spent more time at the office"?

—ANONYMOUS

let's hear it for fathers!

Day one

Mind-Renewal Thought

A Dad's First Priority

You must commit yourselves wholeheartedly to these commands I am giving you. . . . Repeat them again and again to your children. Talk about them when you are at home and when you are away on a journey, when you are lying down and when you are getting up again. . . . Write them on the doorposts of your house and on your gates.

Deuteronomy 6:6-7, 9

Thinking It Over

Every man wants to leave an inheritance. Even poor fathers who lead godly lives can leave a rich legacy of moral values and knowledge about God. Children are full of questions. As indicated in the Scripture above, life with them is full of moments when they are teachable, open to insightful spiritual talk. Wise dads will be on the lookout for these. When you and your child view a sky full of stars, call his attention to the vastness of the universe and the power it must have taken to place all those lights in the sky and to keep track of them by name as the Bible says God does.

Look for times to teach your children about the nature and works of God.

TAKEAWAY

According to the Christian values which govern my life, my most important reason for living is to get the baton—the gospel—safely in the hands of my children. My number one responsibility is to evangelize my own children.

—Dr. James C. Dobson (1936–)

Day
two

Mind-Renewal Thought

Disciplining Kids

Discipline your children while there is hope.
If you don't, you will ruin their lives.
PROVERBS 19:18

Thinking It Over

"The Hebrew word for parents is *horim,* and it comes from the same root as *moreh,* teacher. The parent is, and remains, the first and most important teacher that the child will ever have," says Rabbi Kassel Abelson. Good teachers do not always express love and compassion by withholding punishment. Many fathers have stumbled at this point. Too often, a dad's firmness about enforcing rules goes out the window because he cannot tolerate the resentment and hatred that can come from kids who have been chastised. Is that you? Best to get over it because fair discipline comes with the job of raising good and godly kids. Eventually, your children will thank you for keeping them on a good path. A good book for learning about disciplining your children is *The New Dare to Discipline* by Dr. James Dobson.

TAKEAWAY

The Christian home is the Master's workshop where the processes of character molding are silently, lovingly, faithfully and successfully carried on.

—Richard Monckton Milnes (1809–1885)

Mind-Renewal Thought

God's Promises about Outside Influences on Children's Lives

Teach your children to choose the right path, and when they are older, they will remain upon it.

PROVERBS 22:6

Thinking It Over

Heavenly Father, give me the time and ability to teach my children the right path. So often I get caught up in the urgency of the moment and don't take the time to teach my children. I want them to know what the right path is. I claim your promise to help me. In Jesus' name, amen.

TAKEAWAY

Not a few dads (and moms) are prone to give their children everything except the one thing they need most. That is time: time for listening, time for understanding, time for helping, and time for guiding. It sounds simple, but in reality it is the most difficult and the most sacrificial task of parenthood.

—Emma K. Hulburt

Mind-Renewal Thought

Prime Resource: Praying for My Children

When you pray, go away by yourself, shut the door behind you, and pray to your Father secretly. . . . Your Father knows exactly what you need even before you ask him! Pray like this: . . . "Don't let [my children] yield to temptation, but deliver [them] from the evil one."

MATTHEW 6:6, 8-9, 13

Thinking It Over

Frustration and *worry* are perhaps suitable substitute words for fathering. The job sometimes seems overwhelming. God has promised to give strength, help, and confidence. But how can he answer prayers for help that are not prayed? And how can today's busy father pray if he does not set aside a definite time each day to bring his children before the Lord? When is your prayer time? Do you have one? Maybe this is the day to revise your schedule so it includes a specific time to pray for your family. Many men choose early morning hours when the house is quiet even though it takes getting out of bed before anyone else is up and about. Try it. Then watch for results in your children's lives.

TAKEAWAY

Here are some Bible prayers you can use to pray for your children. Use them to guide you in your prayer time for your family.

> *Holy Father, keep them and care for them—all those you have given me. . . . I'm not asking you to take them out of the world, but to keep them safe from the evil one. . . . Make them pure and holy by teaching them your words of truth.* (John 17:11, 15, 17)

> *May the Lord make you increase and abound in love.* (1 Thessalonians 3:12, NRSV)

I fall to my knees and pray to the Father. . . . I pray that from his glorious, unlimited resources he will give you mighty inner strength through his Holy Spirit. And I pray that Christ will be more and more at home in your hearts as you trust in him. May your roots go down deep into the soil of God's marvelous love. And may you have the power to understand, as all God's people should, how wide, how long, how high, and how deep his love really is. (Ephesians 3:14, 16-18)

Day five

Mind-Renewal Thought

Fathers as Models for Their Children

Be ye doers of the word, and not hearers only, deceiving your own selves.

JAMES 1:22, KJV

Thinking It Over

"Every child has a right to be both well fed and well led," some very wise person has said. Kids *will* copy adults, so dads must address the issue of who is Lord of their lives. Fathers who want their kids to mature into strong, mature men and women of God need to take a good, hard look at themselves to see if some of their own behaviors and attitudes need fixing, like deleting words from their vocabulary that do not reflect the love of Christ or confessing and stopping a particular bad habit. Men who want to be good models for their kids can start by praying this prayer: "Search me, O God, and know my heart; test me and know my thoughts. Point out anything in me that offends you, and lead me along the path of everlasting life." (Psalm 139:23-24)

TAKEAWAY

Children seldom misquote you. They more often repeat word for word what you shouldn't have said.

—Mae Maloo

Day.
SIX

Mind-Renewal Thought

Enjoying Your Children

Children are a gift from the Lord; they are a reward from him. Children born to a young man are like sharp arrows in a warrior's hands. How happy is the man whose quiver is full of them!

PSALM 127:3-5

Thinking It Over

Almost every man seems extremely busy these days. It is hard to find time to provide for his children, to say nothing of actually enjoying them. Understandably, an overworked and harried dad yearns for time for himself. Consequently, lively and demanding children can easily become a burden, instead of a blessing. Feelings of tenderness often get replaced with irritation when children become a challenge to patience and pocketbook. Yet, God has arranged things so that mind and spirit are healed by being with children. A child's giggle or quaint sayings can bring a smile and rejuvenate the heart of almost anyone. One father said, "When I come home from work and hear those little voices shout, 'Daddy's home,' then everything in my world seems all right again, even if my workday went all wrong." Think about the heartache in the many homes that have no children yet yearn for them. Have you considered the awesome potential in each of your children as well as the comfort they can be in old age when they can function as sharp arrows to protect their parents? How about turning off the TV and tossing a basketball with your kids tonight? Have you read your children a story lately? When was the last hug or camping trip?

TAKEAWAY

People always involved in broad issues generally neglect those closest to them. I have seen too many damaged children whose parents were leaders.

—Bruno Bettelheim (1903–1990)

Day seven

Mind-Renewal Thought

Father as Spiritual Head of the Family

We will not hide these truths from our children but will tell the next generation about the glorious deeds of the Lord. We will tell of his power and the mighty miracles he did. . . . He commanded our ancestors to teach them to their children, so the next generation might know them—even the children not yet born—that they in turn might teach their children. So each generation can set its hope anew on God.

PSALM 78:4-7

Thinking It Over

Experts say that by the time children are five, dads and moms will have done at least half of all that can ever be done to determine their children's future faith. Researcher George Barna says that teens have a 32 percent chance of accepting Christ; whereas, the chances of someone over eighteen accepting Christ is a mere 6 percent. The role of the father as the family's spiritual head is a vital one, especially as the culture becomes more and more hostile to faith, often going out of its way to belittle or openly attack Christianity. Today's father has resources available to lead his family in the faith. You can do it even if your dad didn't, even if you don't feel quite capable of taking the reins of spiritual leadership in your home. There *is* help for teaching children about the God to whom they are responsible. They need something to believe in, a sense of purpose in life and hope, even in the darkest circumstances. Yes, it will take effort (do you lead a regular devotional time with your family?); and yes, it will sometimes be inconvenient; and yes, young people may resent taking the time from their busy schedules. But raising wise and godly children will later be a cause of great joy for the dad who is the spiritual leader of his family.

TAKEAWAY

When was the last time that your children saw you on your knees with an open Bible seeking direction from God? That is an unmistakable lesson to a child.

—Dr. Charles Stanley

POWERTHOUGHT

The father and mother of an unnoticed family who, in their seclusion, awaken the mind of one child to the idea and love of goodness, who awaken in him a strength of will to repel temptation, and who send him out prepared to profit by the conflicts of life, surpass in influence a Napoleon breaking the world to his sway.

—William Ellery Channing (1780–1842)

a man and his money

Day one

Mind-Renewal Thought

How Much Money Is Enough?

Those who love money will never have enough. How absurd to think that wealth brings true happiness!

ECCLESIASTES 5:10

Thinking It Over

When asked how much money is enough, John Rockefeller is said to have replied, "Just a little bit more." That is generally how we think in terms of wealth. Instead of craving more and more, doesn't it make sense for a man to stop comparing his lot to everybody else's and to just be content with whatever he has been given, then use it wisely?

TAKEAWAY

When you look at others with their lands and gold,
Think that Christ has promised you his wealth
untold;
Count your many blessings, money cannot buy
Your reward in heaven, nor your home on high.

—Johnson Oatman Jr. (1856–1926)

Mind-Renewal Thought

When You Worry about Money

Look at the birds. They don't need to plant or harvest or put food in barns because your heavenly Father feeds them. And you are far more valuable to him than they are. . . . Your heavenly Father already knows all your needs, and he will give you all you need from day to day if you live for him and make the Kingdom of God your primary concern.

MATTHEW 6:26, 32-33

Thinking It Over

Resolved: I will ask myself, "Is my confidence placed in God himself or in his blessings?" I will stop worrying about money and possessions and start trusting God to provide.

TAKEAWAY

Money has the power, spiritual power, to win our hearts. Behind our coins and dollar bills, or whatever material form we choose to give our money, are spiritual forces.

—Richard J. Foster (1942–)

Day three

Mind-Renewal Thought

Rich Man, Poor Man: Who Is Wealthy? Who Is Poor?

[Jesus speaking] Real life is not measured by how much we own.

Luke 12:15

Thinking It Over

Feeling poor? Despite money problems, maybe your cup is overflowing with rich blessings that you don't very often think about. List below every blessing that comes to mind. Do you have good friends? a godly spouse? healthy children? a comfortable home? bonus benefits like a washer, dryer, microwave? eyes to see and ears to hear? a car? trees and flowers? a job?

1.

2.

3.

4.

5.

Now thank God for each of these.

TAKEAWAY

I have never been poor, only broke. Being poor is a frame of mind. Being broke is only a temporary situation.

—Michael Todd (1909–1958)

Mind-Renewal Thought

So You Want to Be Wealthy?

People who long to be rich fall into temptation and are trapped by many foolish and harmful desires that plunge them into ruin and destruction. For the love of money is at the root of all kinds of evil. And some people, craving money, have wandered from the faith and pierced themselves with many sorrows. But you . . . belong to God.

1 TIMOTHY 6:9-11

Thinking It Over

Materialism runs rampant in our society today. For many the pursuit of money has quickly become the essence of existence and replaced God. Parents who don't need to, have relinquished their role of child care to strangers in order to have a bigger house and more "things."

Belongings never bring the happiness they promise. Even worse, materialism and pursuit of wealth often keep us from producing spiritual fruit: "All too quickly the message is crowded out by the cares of this life, the lure of wealth, and the desire for nice things, so no crop is produced" (Mark 4:19).

TAKEAWAY

In our rich consumer's civilization we spin cocoons around ourselves and get possessed by our possessions.

—Max Lerner

Day five

Mind-Renewal Thought

What We Value Most

You must each make up your own mind as to how much you should give. Don't give reluctantly or in response to pressure. For God loves the person who gives cheerfully.

2 CORINTHIANS 9:7

Thinking It Over

How a man handles money reveals the condition of his soul. Did you know that Jesus talked about money and possessions more than anything else? He knew that riches, or pursuit of them, can take over and control a man's life—but not so likely if wealth is shared. Giving money to God's purposes focuses a man's attention on his Maker as provider of all and shows where his allegiance lies. It is better to think of money in terms of how much good it can do instead of how many good things it can buy. Are you remembering that everything, yes everything, you have comes from God's hand?

TAKEAWAY

There is tremendous freedom of mind in knowing and believing that God owns it all and that money is a resource provided by God to allow us to accomplish his purposes on this earth.

—Ron Blue

Day.
SIX

Mind-Renewal Thoughts

Don't store up treasures here on earth, where they can be eaten by moths and get rusty, and where thieves break in and steal. Store your treasures in heaven, where they will never become moth-eaten or rusty and where they will be safe from thieves.

MATTHEW 6:19-20

Thinking It Over

Money never made a man happy yet, nor will it. There is nothing in its nature to produce happiness. The more a man has, the more he wants. Instead of its filling a vacuum, it makes one. If it satisfies one want, it doubles and triples that want another way. That was a true proverb of the wise man; rely upon it: "Better is little with the fear of the Lord, than great treasure, and trouble therewith."

—Benjamin Franklin (1706–1790)

Anyone who thinks money is everything has never been sick.

—Malcolm S. Forbes (1919–1990)

Day seven

Mind-Renewal Thought

Having More Than Enough

Never think that it was your own strength and energy that made you wealthy. Always remember that it is the Lord your God who gives you power to become rich.

DEUTERONOMY 8:17-18

Thinking It Over

If a person gets his attitude toward money straight, it will help straighten out almost every other area in his life.

—Billy Graham (1918–)

TAKEAWAY

We can stand affliction better than we can prosperity, for in prosperity, we forget God.

—D. L. Moody (1837–1899)

POWERTHOUGHT

No man can tell whether he is rich or poor by turning to his ledger. It is the heart that makes a man rich. He is rich according to what he is, not according to what he has.

—Henry Ward Beecher (1813–1887)

men at work

Day
one

Mind-Renewal Thought

Improving Your Job Outlook

Obey your earthly masters in everything you do. Try to please them all the time, not just when they are watching you. . . . Work hard and cheerfully at whatever you do, as though you were working for the Lord rather than for people. Remember that the Lord will give you an inheritance as your reward, and the Master you are serving is Christ.

COLOSSIANS 3:22-24

Thinking It Over

Three men working on a building site were asked what they were doing. One said, "I'm earning a living." The second said, "I'm filling this truck with dirt and dropping it over there." The third said, "I'm building a cathedral for the glory of God." All three answered accurately, but their perceptions of their work varied widely, stimulating them to look at their work through new eyes.

—*Daily Study Bible for Men*

TAKEAWAY

Work! God wills it. That, it seems to me, is clear.

—Gustave Flaubert (1821–1880)

Mind-Renewal Thought

The Joy of Work

There is nothing better for people than
to be happy in their work.

ECCLESIASTES 3:22

Thinking It Over

The best things are nearest: breath in your nostrils, light in your eyes, flowers at your feet, duties at your hand, the path of God just before you. Then do not grasp at the stars, but do life's plain, common work as it comes.

—Robert Louis Stevenson (1850–1894)

TAKEAWAY

Give us, oh, give us, the man who sings at his work! He will do more in the same time, he will do it better, he will persevere longer. One is scarcely sensible of fatigue while he marches to music. The very stars are said to make harmony as they revolve in their spheres. Wondrous is the strength of cheerfulness, altogether past calculation in its powers of endurance. Efforts, to be permanently useful, must be uniformly joyous, a spirit all sunshine, graceful from very gladness, beautiful because bright.

—Thomas Carlyle (1795–1881)

Mind-Renewal Thought

Climbing the Corporate Ladder

In everything you do, put God first, and he will direct you and crown your efforts with success.

PROVERBS 3:6, TLB

Thinking It Over

It is not what we do that matters, but what a sovereign God chooses to do through us. God doesn't want our success; he wants us. He doesn't demand our achievements; he demands our obedience.

—Charles Colson (1931–)

TAKEAWAY

Success is to be measured not so much by the position that one has reached in life as by the obstacles which he has overcome while trying to succeed.

—Booker T. Washington (1856–1915)

Mind-Renewal Thought

Comfort for Being Laid Off or Changing Jobs

The steps of the godly are directed by the Lord.
He delights in every detail of their lives.
Though they stumble, they will not fall,
for the Lord holds them by the hand.

PSALM 37:23-24

Thinking It Over

Being between jobs is hard on a man's self-esteem. Often confidence goes out the window. Yet, the position you hold (or don't hold) at work has nothing to do with how God sees you. If your job vanishes, you don't. God cares no more, no less for the man who holds an important post than he does for the one who has been given a pink slip, the man who is searching for a new job, or the person who is thinking of leaving because he dislikes his current job. God's love for his own is unchanging, day after day, hour after hour. Every believing man remains God's chosen child, brother to his Son, Jesus Christ, loved fully as much as the Son, a gift to God that he delights in—and much more.

Knowing who he is in the Lord and trusting God in everything helps a man keep his life in balance. If you are feeling down on yourself, read the previous verses over and over until their truth sinks into the innermost core of your being. For other spirit lifters, read Ephesians 1–3 and Colossians 2:8-10.

TAKEAWAY

It is a fact of Christian experience that life is a series of troughs and peaks. In his efforts to get permanent possession of a soul, God relies on the troughs more than the peaks. And some of his special favorites have gone through longer and deeper troughs than anyone else.

—Dr. Peter Marshall (1902–1949)

Mind-Renewal Thought

Humble yourselves under the mighty hand of God, that He may exalt you in due time.

1 PETER 5:6-7, NKJV

Thinking It Over

The day returns and brings us the petty round of irritating concerns and duties. Help us to play the man, help us to perform them with laughter and kind faces, let cheerfulness abound with industry. Give us to go blithely on our business all this day, bring us to our resting beds weary and content and undishonored, and grant us in the end the gift of sleep.

—Robert Louis Stevenson (1850–1894)

TAKEAWAY

A Bad Day at Work

Finish every day and be done with it. For manners and for wise living it is a vice to remember. You have done what you could. Some blunders and absurdities no doubt crept in; forget them as soon as you can. Tomorrow is a new day; you shall begin it well and serenely, and with too high a spirit to be cumbered with your old nonsense. This day is for all that is good and fair. It is too dear, with its hopes and invitations, to waste a moment on the rotten yesterdays.

—Ralph Waldo Emerson (1803–1882)

Day.
SIX

Mind-Renewal Thought

So, You're Succeeding

Whatever I am now, it is all because God poured out his special favor on me.

1 CORINTHIANS 15:10

Thinking It Over

Someone has said, "When you drink water, remember the spring." Never achieve success without giving God the praise because it comes from him. There is a healthy satisfaction in achieving something that includes thanksgiving to God for what he has done through us. Arrogant men glorify themselves by thinking that they alone are solely accountable for their accomplishments.

TAKEAWAY

Have a sincere desire to serve God and mankind, and stop doubting, stop thinking negatively. . . . Simply start living by faith, pray earnestly and humbly, and get into the habit of looking expectantly for the best. . . . When you live on a faith basis, your desire will be only for that which you can ask in God's name. . . . By success, of course, I do not mean that you may become rich, famous, or powerful. . . . I mean the development of mature and constructive personality.

—Dr. Norman Vincent Peale (1898–1993)

Day
seven

Mind-Renewal Thought

Integrity in the Workplace

Dear brothers and sisters, you are foreigners and aliens here. . . . Be careful how you live among your unbelieving neighbors. Even if they accuse you of doing wrong, they will see your honorable behavior, and they will believe and give honor to God.

1 PETER 2:11-12

Thinking It Over

Every job is a self-portrait of the man who does it. It is a revelation of his inner life, not only to others, but to himself. Being God's man involves doing a job with excellence. The behavior of lazy or self-indulgent workers who claim to be believers speaks poorly of their Lord. The gospel can be hindered by a Christian man who does not build a reputation of integrity, honesty, and a job well done. Sometimes the choice is between what is popular and comfortable and what is right and true. Virtuous conduct at work may not always lead to popularity and more profit, but it allows others to see the good in a man and perhaps recognize where it came from. Some may even come to know the Lord because of a coworker who is a man of principle.

TAKEAWAY

The most important qualities of life—a life of integrity, a strong work ethic, treating people with dignity—arise out of the changeless core that is constantly reenergized in the presence of God.

—Wayne Schmidt

POWERTHOUGHT

Whatever you are, be a good one.

—Abraham Lincoln (1809–1865)

when your world falls apart

Day one

Mind-Renewal Thought

Maybe You Feel Like This Today

Is it nothing to you, all you who pass by? Look around and see if there is any suffering like mine. . . . I weep; tears flow down my cheeks. No one is here to comfort me; any who might encourage me are far away. . . . My heart is broken and my soul despairs. . . . My groans are many, and my heart is faint.

LAMENTATIONS 1:12, 16, 20, 22

Thinking It Over

In our society men are often afraid they will not be "man enough." Strong men often think that human responses like fear, doubt, and anger in the midst of painful circumstances are cause for shame. Perhaps you can't keep from crying out in your misery and even feel humiliated about shedding tears and asking, "God, where are you?" There is comfort in the fact that a very human Jesus responded to his own terrible torment with loud cries and trembling that seem to parallel those of distraught men today. You will not feel so embarrassed if you remember Jesus. He too felt agony— so much that he literally sweat blood. He too cried out in despair, "Father, why have you forsaken me?" Yet, not long after came the Resurrection and the wonderful consequences that followed for humanity.

TAKEAWAY

To be commanded to love God at all, let alone in the wilderness, is like being commanded to be well when we are sick, to sing for joy when we are dying of thirst, to run when our legs are broken. But this is the first and great commandment nonetheless. Even in the wilderness—especially in the wilderness—you shall love him.

—Frederick Buechner (1926–)

Mind-Renewal Thought

Why am I discouraged? Why so sad?
I will put my hope in God!

PSALM 43:5

Thinking It Over

Faith isn't really faith until it's all that you are holding on to.

—Tim Hansel

TAKEAWAY

Great is Thy faithfulness, O God my Father,
There is no shadow of turning with Thee;
Thou changest not, Thy compassions they fail not;
As Thou hast been Thou forever wilt be.

—Thomas Obadiah Chisholm (1866–1960)

Day three

Mind-Renewal Thought

What God Wants When Trouble Comes

Trust me in your times of trouble, and I will rescue you, and you will give me glory.

PSALM 50:15

Thinking It Over

Troubles are often the tools by which God fashions us for better things.

—Henry Ward Beecher (1813–1887)

TAKEAWAY 

God, in my pain and distress, I have changed my view of you because you are turning out to be much more than I ever dared imagine, infinitely beyond my highest hopes and dreams. Now I believe you when you said, "I know the plans I have for you. . . . They are plans for good and not for disaster" (Jeremiah 29:11).

—Journal entry of an injured woman three months after being hurt in a bad accident

Mind-Renewal Thought

Help for Those at the End of Their "Strength" Rope

Even when we are too weak to have any faith left, he remains faithful to us and will help us, for he cannot disown us who are part of himself, and he will always carry out his promises to us.

2 TIMOTHY 2:13,TLB

Thinking It Over

You are strong in the Lord's strength. Your confidence must not be in the church, your pastor, your spouse, your Bible study group, or the godly person who discipled you. This doesn't mean you *feel* God's strength come over you. You don't gain God's strength. You *have* it. His strength is Christ in you. Notice the Scripture [Ephesians 6:10, NIV] doesn't say we are to *become* strong, it says, "*be* strong." Strong is something you *are,* not something you become. When God says "Be strong," it isn't the same as being told as a child, "Big boys don't cry." It is a loving exhortation, a reminder of the facts—"Be strong in my strength which dwells in you."

—Preston Gillham

TAKEAWAY 

Simply trusting every day,
Trusting through a stormy way;
Even when my faith is small,
Trusting Jesus, that is all.

Trusting as the moments fly,
Trusting as the days go by;
Trusting Him whate'er befall,
Trusting Jesus, that is all.

—Edgar Page Stites (1836–1921)

Day five

Mind-Renewal Thought

Hope for Discouraged Men

I am the Lord, the God of all the peoples of the world. Is anything too hard for me?

JEREMIAH 32:27

Thinking It Over

If God be God, then no insoluble problems exist. And if God be *my* God, then no problem of mine is without its appropriate solution.

—Maurice Roberts

TAKEAWAY

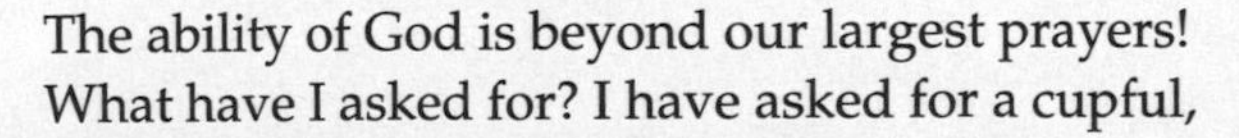

The ability of God is beyond our largest prayers! What have I asked for? I have asked for a cupful, and the ocean remains! I have asked for a sunbeam, and the sun abides! My best asking falls immeasurably short of my Father's giving: it is beyond all that we can ask.

—John Henry Jowett (1864–1923)

Day.
SIX

Mind-Renewal Thought

From Paul, Whose World Was Crumbling

The first time I was brought before the judge, no one was with me. Everyone had abandoned me. . . . But the Lord stood with me and gave me strength. . . . And he saved me from certain death. . . . To God be the glory forever and ever. Amen.

2 TIMOTHY 4:16-18

Thinking It Over

Adversity itself is not the issue; what you learn through the disasters of life is the issue. God did not love Paul any less when he was whipped, beaten, imprisoned, and stoned, nor did he withhold help when Paul was brought before the court of Nero. When the court scene was all over, Paul discovered that he had learned much about God and realized that his heavenly Father had been there all the time constructing the events in Paul's favor and revealing his faithfulness. "Meeting God in our trials is better than getting out of them," says Gale Fields. Have you been asking God what he is going to do? He will never tell you. God does not tell you what he is going to do; he reveals *who he is*.

TAKEAWAY

I pray God may open your eyes and let you see what hidden treasures he bestows on us in the trials from which the world thinks only to flee.

—John of Avila (1500–1569)

Day
seven

Mind-Renewal Thought

Whenever trouble comes your way, let it be an opportunity for joy. For when your faith is tested, your endurance has a chance to grow. So let it grow, for when your endurance is fully developed, you will be strong in character and ready for anything.

James 1:2-4

Thinking It Over

Surviving Difficult Times

The key to handling suffering and trials is to see them from God's perspective. So often we let trials make us bitter, when God's purpose is to make us better. Contentment depends on our focus, not on the trial itself. If we are focusing on God and what he is trying to do through our lives, we can endure suffering. If we are focusing on our circumstances, we become bitter, angry, and defeated.

Our dogs, Molly and Muffit, are good examples. They spend most of their time in the backyard or in the house or in the car, but once in a while we put a leash on them and go for a walk. They pull, choke, strain, cough, and struggle. They would have a much happier walk if they would just relax and work within the "trial." That's a picture of us. We choke, struggle, and strain against the trial and have a miserable time.

—Chuck Snyder, *The Taming of a Type "A" Male*

TAKEAWAY

When we assume God is working for our best, and we relax and try to fit into His plans, things go much smoother for us.

—Chuck Snyder, *The Taming of a Type "A" Male*

POWERTHOUGHT

The only way to meet affliction is to pass through it solemnly, slowly, with humility, and faith, as the Israelites passed through the Red Sea (they just trusted God and kept walking forward in the ever deeper water as though they were on dry ground even though it looked like the huge waves would drown them). If we keep on keeping on, the very waves of misery will divide and become to us a wall, one on the right side and one the left, until the gulf narrows before our eyes, and we land safe on the opposite shore.

—Dinah Maria Mulock Craik (1826–1887)

men growing older, men growing wiser

Day one

Mind-Renewal Thought

God's Rules for Aging Gracefully

When people live to be very old, let them rejoice in every day of life.

ECCLESIASTES 11:8

Thinking It Over

"Old age is like a plane flying through a storm. Once aboard, there is nothing you can do," said Golda Meir. Few people relish getting older, but since aging is as much a normal season of a man's life as any other, it is important that men growing older refrain from yearning for past things. Sure, a man in middle years and beyond may not have the strength, endurance, or physical attractiveness of his youth, but if he knows God, he stands as a living testimony to his heavenly Father's trustworthiness. And he can say so. Rather than lamenting about limited years remaining, he can become a self-encourager by thanking God for being faithful through the multitude of happenings over the years. Unlike those who are yet young, an older man can remember many instances of God's past goodness and guidance.

Think about it. Despite tough times, through wonderful times, you have arrived safely! Let your heart rejoice! Perhaps others will be encouraged, even willing, to hear your personal testimony of God's faithfulness through every term of life and your deliberate choice to trust him in years ahead.

TAKEAWAY

Spiritual maturity is the point at which we cease to rationalize our faults and begin to symbolize our faith.

—Albert M. Wells

Mind-Renewal Thought

The Benefits of Growing Older

Wisdom belongs to the aged, and understanding to those who have lived many years.

JOB 12:12

Thinking It Over

Because older people know more about the world and themselves, they develop a renewed ability to handle daily stresses and gain a greater sense of self-confidence. And aging leads to an increase in what psychologists now call crystallized intelligence—a capacity to apply knowledge to real-life situations—what was once called wisdom.

—*The Bottom Line*

TAKEAWAY

Time will teach more than all our thoughts.

—Benjamin Disraeli (1804–1881)

Day three

Mind-Renewal Thought

When You Hate Having Wrinkles and Graying Hair

The Lord said . . . , "Don't judge by his appearance or height. . . . The Lord doesn't make decisions the way you do! People judge by outward appearance, but the Lord looks at a person's thoughts and intentions."

1 SAMUEL 16:7

Thinking It Over

A man should not judge his worth by appearance, height, complexion, hair color, vocation, education, achievements, or any other outward criteria devised by others. The Lord doesn't, so why should you? What is more important is a godly character developed from following Christ. The resulting fruit is joy, peace, patience, kindness, gentleness, and self-control, which will last far longer than your good looks, figure, or macho muscles.

Give no one praise for their beauty; think less of no one for their appearance.

—*Wisdom of Ben Siva*

Mind-Renewal Thought

Aging in a World with Diminished Respect for Seniors

I am mocked by those who are younger than I.

JOB 30:1

Thinking It Over

Jesus, still lead on,
Till our rest be won;
Heav'nly Leader, still direct us,
Still support, console, protect us,
Till we safely stand
In our fatherland!

—Count Nikolaus L. von Zinzendorf (1700–1760)

TAKEAWAY

We are the miracles, the great inscrutable mystery of God.

—Thomas Carlyle (1795–1881)

Mind-Renewal Thought

Encourager for Men Growing Older

The love of the Lord remains forever with those who fear him. His salvation extends to the children's children of those who are faithful to his covenant, of those who obey his commandments!

PSALM 103:17-18

Thinking It Over

Watch where Jesus went. The one dominant note in his life was to do his Father's will. His is not the way of wisdom or of success, but the way of faithfulness.

—Oswald Chambers (1874–1917)

TAKEAWAY

Green pastures are before me,
Which yet I have not seen;
Bright skies will soon be o'er me,
Where the dark clouds have been:
My life I cannot measure,
The path of life is free;
My Savior has my treasure,
And he will walk with me.

—Anna L. Waring (1823–1910)

Day. SIX

Mind-Renewal Thought

Prayers for Growing Older

[Lord,] don't let those who trust in you stumble because of me.

PSALM 69:6

Thinking It Over

Lord, in a world that worships youthfulness and overachievement, I thank you for the ability to see life in a different way. I thank you for the seasons that make time so rich and full of discovery. I am grateful that so many of the saints in history, and especially in Scripture, were clearly beyond retirement age when they made important contributions to your kingdom. Open my eyes to see all that you have planned for this phase of life. Fill my heart with great expectation and confidence and a willingness to continue to hear your voice and follow where you lead. I ask for bodily and mental strength, and for continued grace and growing contentment, so that my light may shine in a world full of bitterness and wasted abilities. Amen.

—*Family Prayers for All Occasions*

TAKEAWAY

We are, after all, like lumps of clay.
There are brittle pieces, hard pieces.
We have little shape or beauty.
But we need not despair.
If we are clay, let us remember there is a Potter, and His wheel.

—Dr. Peter Marshall (1902–1949)

Day
seven

Mind-Renewal Thought

A Fear of Growing Older

I created you and have cared for you since before you were born. I will be your God throughout your lifetime—until your hair is white with age. I made you, and I will care for you. I will carry you along.

ISAIAH 46:3-4

Thinking It Over

Did you take note of the phrase above: "Since *before* you were born"? Think about God watching over and protecting you before you ever made entrance into this world, while you were growing inside your mother. Think about it! Even then! So, why would you have any doubts about his loving care just because your hair is graying at the temples or your strength is beginning to fade? God continues his watch no matter what your age. You can relax in his care. Claim this promise: "The Lord keeps watch over you as you come and go, both now and forever" (Psalm 121:8).

TAKEAWAY

Don't try to hold God's hand; let Him hold yours. Let Him do the holding, and you the trusting.

—Hammer William Webb-Peploe (1837–1923)

POWERTHOUGHT

No wise man ever wished to be younger.

—Jonathan Swift (1667–1745)

i've strayed: will god take me back?

Day one

Mind-Renewal Thought

For the Man Who Wants to
Come Back to God:

The Lord still waits for you to come to him so he can show you his love and compassion. For the Lord is a faithful God.

ISAIAH 30:18

Thinking It Over

The big picture is simply this: People turn their backs on God and God immediately goes to work to regain fellowship.

—Dr. Charles Stanley

TAKEAWAY

Thou hast made us for thyself, and the heart of man is restless until it finds its rest in thee.

—St. Augustine (354–430)

Mind-Renewal Thought

God's Invitation

This is what the Lord says . . . : "Come back to me and live!"

Amos 5:4

Thinking It Over

Life really isn't as troublesome, overwhelming, and confusing as we at times make it out to be. The answer: Just run home to God. Admit whatever waywardness there has been, and recall the great love that sent Jesus to die on a cross for your sins. That kind of love never lets you go. The Hound of Heaven has been trailing you all the while you have been away. And you never knew! Some ask, "Will God love and accept me as much as before I left him behind?" Yes! Come on home to God! He will welcome you with open arms just as the Prodigal Son was welcomed by his father. Come back with repentance for straying away and forgive yourself with the biblical reminder that "all of us have strayed away like sheep. We have left God's paths to follow our own" (Isaiah 53:6).

TAKEAWAY 

"Not to decide is to decide" may be a common saying, but it is true. To hear the shepherd's voice and shut ourselves to the sound is spiritually dangerous.

—Leighton Ford

Day three

Mind-Renewal Thought

Why Do Men Abandon God? Here Are God's Answers:

Only fools say in their hearts, "There is no God." They are corrupt and their actions are evil.

PSALM 14:1-2

Thinking It Over

Closed spiritual eyes blind men to God, as do independence and self-sufficiency, especially if they are unusually gifted or blessed materially. Such men often feel things are going well enough without having anything spiritual in their lives. They want to be their own masters. But, without knowing the true God, men, young or old, will find other gods to replace him in their hearts. In their own supposed adequacy, many will deny a need for God and go overboard to place their affections on other things like money, career, music, friends, hobbies, even television. Later, such men often become disillusioned with this self-imposed "good life," realizing that it lacks depth and purpose.

Sometimes it takes a major or minor catastrophe to bring a man back to God. But once he gets over the foolishness of trying to run the course of life alone and admits his own emptiness, he can acknowledge the One who created everything and reveals himself (in both nature and Scripture) to anyone who is searching. When a man sees his waywardness and cries out with deep repentance for forgiveness, God hears and answers.

TAKEAWAY

What are you going to do with Jesus? . . . If Christ were to reappear—dressed in a modern business suit—on Main Street or Madison Avenue, would we react any differently than the inhabitants of Jerusalem in A.D. 32? Would we have enough dedication and stamina to accept him and his audacious claims, to make known our allegiance to him under the pressure of an unpopular cause and ostracism? The sad truth is that purity and sacrifice are unpopular in every century.

—Dr. Peter Marshall (1903–1949)

Mind-Renewal Thought

God's Invitation

You don't love me or each other as you did at first! . . . Turn back to me again.

REVELATION 2:4-5

Thinking It Over

Why Men Return to God

It was Sunday and the son was having a streak of rebellion against God and church. "Dad, when am I going to be old enough not to have to go to church like you?" asked the boy. The father looked a long moment at his precious son, hesitated, and then wisely said, "Wait a minute, Son, and I will get dressed and go with you."

TAKEAWAY

O Love that wilt not let me go,
I rest my weary soul in Thee;
I give Thee back the life I owe,
That in Thine ocean depths its flow
May richer, fuller be.

—George Matheson (1842–1906)

Mind-Renewal Thought

God's Invitation

Don't you realize how kind, tolerant, and patient God is with you? Can't you see how kind he has been in giving you time to turn from your sin?

ROMANS 2:4

Thinking It Over

A Prayer for Returning to God

My soul is sick, my heart is sore,
Now I'm coming home;
My strength renew, my hope restore,
Lord, I'm coming home.

Coming home, coming home,
Nevermore to roam,
Open wide Thine arms of love,
Lord, I'm coming home.

—William J. Kirkpatrick (1838–1921)

TAKEAWAY

Repentance is not something God demands of you before He will take you back. It is simply a description of what going back is like.

—C. S. Lewis (1898–1963)

Mind-Renewal Thought

God's Affirmation That You Are Welcome Back in His Fold

"My wayward children," says the Lord, "come back to me, and I will heal your wayward hearts."

JEREMIAH 3:22

Thinking It Over

Giving Yourself Credit for the Sense to Return

"Men occasionally stumble over the truth, but most pick themselves up and hurry off as if nothing happened," said one unknown writer. But *you* didn't! *You* decided to come back! Take praise for humbling yourself enough to return to your God. It is not an easy thing to do because it takes saying, "I was wrong."

TAKEAWAY

Maybe you are sensing a distance between you and God; perhaps you wonder if he can ever accept you back. Could it be a false feeling of guilt about past sin, even though confessed? Or a feeling that you are not good enough to return to God? What you feel is not real, so get over it. The battle is being waged in your thought life, so reprogram it. Repentant prodigal sons are always welcomed back *with open arms.* You can stand on these facts of God's Word:

> *Whoever comes to me I will never drive away.* (John 6:37, NIV)
>
> *Look! Here I stand at the door and knock. If you hear me calling and open the door, I will come in, and we will share a meal as friends.* (Revelation 3:20)

Mind-Renewal Thought

What's Next, Now That I've Decided to Return to God?

Don't copy the behavior and customs of this world, but be a new and different person with a fresh newness in all you do and think. Then you will learn from your own experience how his ways will really satisfy you.

ROMANS 12:2, TLB

Thinking It Over

You cannot stay where you are and go with God. You cannot continue doing things your way and accomplish God's purposes in His ways. Once you have adjusted your life to God,

His purposes, and His ways, you are prepared to obey Him.

—Henry T. Blackaby and Claude V. King

TAKEAWAY

In our walk with the Lord, we must be aware of other shipwrecked saints who have stopped seeking God. They have given up, quitting on the Lord for one reason or another. In their rebellion they have suffered, become useless, and endangered other well-meaning believers. When we see these people spewing bitterness against God, the church, or other believers, our first reaction is to avoid them. However, the Lord wants to use us—no matter how battered we feel—to help gently pull these shipwrecked saints to safety where they can be restored to God's plan and purpose for their lives.

—*In Touch*

POWERTHOUGHT

God is faithful to restore even the most beaten and battered vessels.

—Anonymous

appendix

Have You Heard of the Four Spiritual Laws?

Just as there are physical laws that govern the physical universe, so are there spiritual laws which govern your relationship with God.

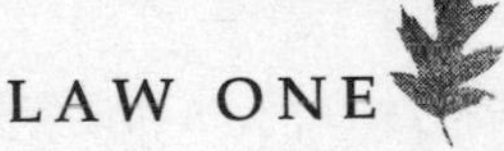

LAW ONE

God **LOVES** you and offers a wonderful **PLAN** for your life.

GOD'S LOVE
"For God so loved the world, that He gave His only begotten Son, that whoever believes in Him should not perish, but have eternal life" (John 3:16).

GOD'S PLAN
(Christ speaking) "I came that they might have life, and might have it abundantly" (that it might be full and meaningful) (John 10:10).

Why is it that most people are not experiencing the abundant life? Because . . .

LAW TWO

Man is **SINFUL** and **SEPARATED** from God.
Thus he cannot know and experience
God's love and plan for his life.

MAN IS SINFUL

"For all have sinned and fall short of the glory of God" (Romans 3:23).

Man was created to have fellowship with God; but because of his stubborn self-will he chose to go his own independent way, and fellowship with God was broken. This self-will, characterized by an attitude of active rebellion or passive indifference, is an evidence of what the Bible calls sin.

MAN IS SEPARATED

"For the wages of sin is death" (spiritual separation from God) (Romans 6:23).

This diagram illustrates that God is holy and man is sinful. A great gulf separates the two. Man is continually trying to reach God and the abundant life through his own efforts, such as a good life, philosophy, or religion.

The Third Law explains the only way to bridge this gulf. . . .

LAW THREE

Jesus Christ is God's ONLY provision for man's sin. Through him you can know and experience God's love and plan for your life.

HE DIED IN OUR PLACE

"But God demonstrates His own love toward us, in that while we were yet sinners, Christ died for us" (Romans 5:8).

HE ROSE FROM THE DEAD

"Christ died for our sins. . . . He was buried. . . . He was raised on the third day, according to the Scriptures. . . . He appeared to Peter, then to the twelve. After that He appeared to more than five hundred" (1 Corinthians 15:3-6).

HE IS THE ONLY WAY TO GOD

"Jesus said to him, 'I am the way, and the truth, and the life; no one comes to the Father, but through Me'" (John 14:6).

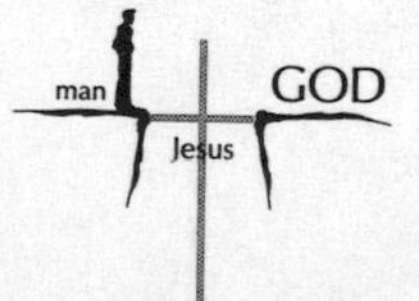

This diagram illustrates that God has bridged the gulf which separates us from Him by sending His Son, Jesus Christ, to die on the cross in our place to pay the penalty for our sins.

It is not enough just to know these three laws. . . .

LAW FOUR

We must individually **RECEIVE** Jesus Christ as Savior and Lord; then we can know and experience God's love and plan for our lives.

WE MUST RECEIVE CHRIST

"But as many as received Him, to them He gave the right to become children of God, even to those who believe in His name" (John 1:12).

WE RECEIVE CHRIST THROUGH FAITH

"For by grace you have been saved through faith; and that not of yourselves, it is the gift of God; not as a result of works, that no one should boast" (Ephesians 2:8-9).

WHEN WE RECEIVE CHRIST, WE EXPERIENCE A NEW BIRTH

(Read John 3:1-8.)

WE RECEIVE CHRIST BY PERSONAL INVITATION

(Christ speaking) "Behold, I stand at the door and knock; if any one hears My voice and opens the door, I will come in to him" (Revelation 3:20).

Receiving Christ involves turning to God from self (repentance) and trusting Christ to come into our lives to forgive our sins and to make us the kind of people He wants us to be. Just to agree intellectually that Jesus Christ is the Son of God and that He died on the cross for our sins is not enough. Nor is it enough to have an emotional experience. We receive Jesus Christ by faith, as an act of the will.

These two circles represent two kinds of lives:

SELF-DIRECTED LIFE

S — Self is on the throne
† — Christ is outside the life
• — Interests are directed by self, often resulting in discord and frustration

CHRIST-DIRECTED LIFE

† — Christ is in the life and on the throne
S — Self is yielding to Christ
• — Interests are directed by Christ, resulting in harmony with God's plan

Which circle best represents your life?
Which circle would you like to have represent your life?

The following explains how you can receive Christ:

YOU CAN RECEIVE CHRIST
RIGHT NOW BY FAITH THROUGH PRAYER
(PRAYER IS TALKING WITH GOD.)

God knows your heart and is not so concerned with your words as He is with the attitude of your heart. The following is a suggested prayer:

"Lord Jesus, I need You. Thank You for dying on the cross for my sins. I open the door of my life and receive You as my Savior and Lord. Thank You for forgiving my sins and giving me eternal life. Take control of the throne of my life. Make me the kind of person You want me to be."

Does this prayer express the desire of your heart? If it does, pray this prayer right now, and Christ will come into your life, as He promised.

About the Author

Alice Chapin has retired from Campus Crusade for Christ Military Ministry staff after twenty-four years. In addition to writing, she has also taught elementary school. She is the author of several books, including *400 Creative Ways to Say I Love You*, *365 Bible Promises*, and *Nine Months and Counting*. She and her husband have four grown daughters and live in Georgia. Alice is a member of the Authors Guild.

Books by Alice Chapin

The Little Book of Big Bible Promises

The Little Book of Big Bible Promises for Women

The Little Book of Big Bible Promises for Seniors

The Little Book of Big Bible Promises for Men

365 Bible Promises for Busy People

365 Bible Promises for Hurting People

365 Bible Promises for People Who Worry

400 Creative Ways to Say I Love You

400 More Creative Ways to Say I Love You

Nine Months & Counting

Reaching Back

Meals in a Muffin

We're Having a New Baby